POLITICS

A *Try It Like This* Book

By

Jarrod Welsh

ISBN: 979-8-9854031-8-3

Cover design by: Melissa Welsh, Cassidy Welsh
Library of Congress Control Number: 1-9538279881
Printed in the United States of America

CONTENTS

FOREWORD

I've heard people say something to the effect that those who seek the presidency are "insane" and, judging from some of the candidates we've seen in recent years, they're partially correct. I say partially because, for a servant of the people, the presidency is, or should be, the pinnacle of service. It's amazing how the presidency has become a job where only the richest and most popular people are elected. "Shouldn't the most popular person be elected?" you ask. Yes, but popular for the right reasons. They should be elected for their actions that illustrate their desire to not only lead but, more importantly, to serve.

I hear what you're saying, "why you?" Well, Lincoln grew up in squalor and used to float a flatboat loaded with produce and cured meat down the Mississippi. Those are some humble beginnings for a President which means that any of us could potentially do it although, unless the

American people come together and abandon the Democrats and Republicans, I'll need to raise about $100 mil to do it.

Also, I have no desire to "go negative" I couldn't care less what the other candidates did or do nor do I care about what they will or won't do for the country. I know that my work ethic, and ambition to make the country better, far surpasses any other candidate. I have no desire to be rich or famous. I have a desire to serve. Some say that's naïve but, without people like me, nothing would get done. I believe in service for many reasons, but most of all I do it because it needs to be done. My mind always comes back to serving others because there are so many that need help. As I've said before, the president is the servant of us all and is actually the least important of us all. For decades we've seen presidents fail resulting in little to no consequences, how could this person be more important than anyone else. If I were to gain the trust of the American people enough to be president, I would not be haughty but humbled by the gesture.

book, kind of. Instead of making life saving medication for those who have/had no control over their affliction (type 1 diabetes in kids, for instance.) free, he suggested making it affordable because, according to him, type 1 diabetes medication is around $500. However, just when I was getting on board, he resorted to a politician's old trick. He said something to the effect of "that's why we need to pass this bill" – and there it is, the disingenuous actions that politicians have mastered. He says something that makes perfect and total sense to everyone and then you find out that he only did it to guilt you into supporting the pork riddled, $1.7 trillion, Build Back Better bill. This is where the true evil lies. I've mentioned it before, but I bring it up again because this is what I'm talking about, the gigantic elephant in the room that is overspending and dishonesty. They tell you a couple of "good" things to mask the countless "bad" things in the bill. Actually, very few people know if the other things in the bill are bad or good because it's 2135 pages long. We already know our elected leaders don't read the entire

ELECTED OFFICIALS AND LEADERS

Our elected officials are living the good life while their constituents are suffering. Not to get too political but it is appalling that no one acknowledges the fact that most, if not all, of the poverty stricken, feces laden, and generally disregarded districts are run by democrats. It's also amazing that the people in those districts continue to elect these officials who are doing nothing for them. This is not to say that republicans are better but at least they are honest about their goals and plans for the country. Republicans come out and say they are for individual freedom and capitalism, which is a thinly veiled way of saying "handle things on your own" (which most of us would prefer – the less government involvement in my life the better) but it seems democrats tell people what they want to hear regardless of how impossible, and preposterous, it sounds. If our elected officials, both democrats and republicans, truly cared about the people they serve, they would be working tirelessly to improve their respective districts/states. Unfortunately, our "lawmakers" focus more on reelection than they ever do on people. Congress is a money-making scheme first and a "service job" a distant second, if at all. Actually, their second function is ensuring their side prevails. This occurs on both sides and is a waste of taxpayer money. How often do we hear about a bill that has no chance of passing yet is presented anyway? This does not serve "we the people" well. The process should be a formality in that before a bill is introduced it should already have bi-partisan buy-in. Representatives and Senators from both sides, and a presidential rep (if not the President himself, depending on the gravity of the bill), should sit in a room and figure out what works best for the people, not just their respective side, and then finalize the proposed bill and introduce it to The House as I said, as a formality. Then it should go to the Senate for concurrence (which should be fast since The Senate had a hand in its formulation/finalization), and then off to the White House for approval. This would expedite the process exponentially and actually help the people of this country.

Habits of Many Politicians

Speaking of those whom the media disingenuously cover, how long are we going to allow politicians to use the same tactics I mentioned above? They speak in soundbites and party talking points for no real reason other than to grandstand for their side. How have we allowed this to go on for so long? We go to the polls and vote and are continuously let down and discouraged. It's time we really tried to hold people accountable for their poor performance. Make these people earn that pension after five years. It's a straight up crime that elected officials are allowed to vote "present" or not at all and still keep their jobs. How is there not a clause that makes them do their job? There is, actually, it's called our vote, but we constantly fail to weed out the riff raff and actually elect servants of the people.

At the time of this writing, President Biden stated something amazing, something I wrote in my second bills so who is writing/reading these things? Who is conducting the quality control? By the time it gets to "we the people" it's already a done deal and we just have to live with whatever's in it.

Why couldn't we just pass a bill that says all type 1 diabetes medication for children will be administered at no cost? That seems like a bill that everyone would support, one that would fly through the house and senate and be ready ASAP for the president to sign. But we don't do that. The disingenuous charlatans "battle" it out, fighting tooth and nail to get their pathetic part of the bill approved so they can be a "hero" to their constituents and get reelected, which is their only goal anyway. Meanwhile the bill stalls and/or gets voted down and sick kids are denied their medicine. We'll know that they get denied their medicine because the president will make sure to shame those who voted against the children while leaving out the parts about overspending and taking care of special interests. Yes, it's amazing what we allow them to perpetrate.

Every bill should be limited to a page or two. It should use bullet statements and have no excess wording. If clarification is needed, then the bill's champion makes himself available to provide it, and we move on. But one side putting in BS and the other side voting against the BS is un-American. Just think how many people our government could actually, really, help if they genuinely had our best interests in mind. Also, It's not like they don't have time to vote on multiple bills.

The answer is, there simply isn't enough time to do what's right and look out for themselves. They must ensure their finances, and future, are secure before they move onto the American people. That's why they begin the campaign for reelection as soon as they are elected. The campaigning never really stops, which is why very little ever gets accomplished. Those "in charge" will always choose their wealth and success over their community, which is why we need independently wealthy people to lead our country.

If you remove the obstructions to true progress (greed, megalomania, and weakness) I believe we'll get the people we need in Washington. Yes, the independently wealthy may have those aforementioned aspects but they've already made their money so they can focus on us, in a perfect world. Also, those wealthy candidates don't have the worry of raising funds to obscure their thinking. But few people like that will run because "we" drag these people through the mud and focus on the wrong things. They'd much rather enjoy their life than have it upended. "We" are our own worst enemy because we allow the media to dissect everyone and explore every bit of minutia, regardless of how relevant it is.

Now, regarding the "top" politician, I'm not sure where it went off the rails, but it really seems like the President is not really in charge. It's blatantly obvious with Biden but it seems like it's been going on for some time now. I can understand how it could happen; the two largest political parties have gained so much power that they each take over the office of the President when their candidate is elected. It actually makes sense with the way the leadership of these two entities think. Surely, they couldn't leave the country in the hands of someone else, only they know how to best run the country to ensure both parties maintain their power, money, and influence. The Presidency has become a sham, a tool for Democrats and Republicans to use for their own selfish reasons. It's not about "America" anymore, it's about money and power and only those aligned with the respective parties benefit from this power. It really is amazing that people can't see how corrupt both parties are, they only need to recognize that neither party has done anything for the betterment of the U.S., at most they do things that give the appearance of helping only their side but the efforts they champion are usually unquantifiable and just make people feel good which garners votes.

In the past it seemed like Presidents actually ran the country and the people that worked for them actually worked for them, not the other way around. I couldn't imagine Washington or Lincoln reading from a card to tell them where to sit or who to address first in a room full of diplomats. But ever since Clinton it seems like someone is "controlling" the President.

Obviously, he has a team of people to tell him when his appointments are or what he's supposed to say and when, but whenever Presidents seem to go "off book" they put their foot squarely in their mouth, as if their personal views don't align with "the party's". I'm sure this is true in most respects. It was always kind of obvious, but Biden has really pulled back the curtain and given us way more than a peek at how much he is controlled by his handlers. This has nothing to do with bipartisan politics, but everything to do with corruption. This is also the reason why the republican party is so fractured over Donald Trump. He actually seemed like he was calling the shots and saying what he wanted, not what he was told. This angered the republican party establishment because they are in charge, and they don't like someone who doesn't "fall in line". This isn't to say that Trump was the best candidate or that he should be President again although, if him being elected means the parties are not in control then I'm all for it. We just need to find someone who is as defiant as Trump but who everyone in the country can support. At this point, Trump is too polarizing and really won't ever unite the country.

This blatantly illustrates how much the two major parties want to control the office of the President. Obama was probably one of the worst examples because, unlike GWB and Biden, he seemed to "be in charge" but was really being paraded around by his party like a rock star instead of like a President. His party also had the unique opportunity to unite people by accentuating his biracialism but instead chose to further divide the country by only focusing on one of his races. This is by design because neither party wants unity among Americans, they want to keep us divided because it is more profitable to them. As I write this, I am becoming infuriated that "We the People" are continuously being manipulated by these two private organizations (democrats and republicans). That "we" can't see that these two criminal entities should be shunned and never allowed to assist another political candidate. After an entity does this much damage to a populace they should be outlawed. Speaking of that, all political parties should be outlawed. A person should run on their own merits, not the corrupt dealings of a political party.

But this is what happens in this world. Something righteous and good, like the beginning of our country and the election of an already established leader like General Washington, has been bastardized by greed and lust for power and has become controlled by those who only care about themselves. And what about that, electing a general to be President? We used to do it quite a bit and it seemed to work relatively well. Instead, we elect politicians who are already corrupted and just continue to be during their term(s). Now, this isn't to say that generals aren't politicians in a uniform, but I'll bet we'd have better luck with a retired military member than a lawyer or lifelong politician.

The bottom line is that the federal government is controlled by either the democrat or republican party, depending on who is in office, and we need to wake up to that fact and vote accordingly. People are afraid to vote against the two parties because they think it will just give the other side a vote but that's only a scare tactic used by the parties to keep you voting for them. We need to stand up to these nefarious organizations and take back our country.

𝔅ills

Speaking of bills presented to Congress, it should be illegal for more than one subject to be included in a bill. Too often unscrupulous Congress members will either try to slip in a "rider" (a provision that has little or nothing to do with the main bill) to try to get the rider approved without anyone knowing or to get the main bill voted down because of the rider attached. A bill should contain one main issue which should be discussed until a workable solution can be achieved. As I mentioned before, representatives from the executive and legislative branches should meet to finalize each bill and stay in that meeting until the work is complete. How many great bills could have been passed if only the proper amount of work had been done? How does Congress justify including unrelated riders? The answer is they don't have to justify it, the law is written to allow it, and no one is doing anything to prevent it or change the law. The horrible thing is that these people know exactly what they're doing and how despicable it really is. They know that if there is a bill introduced that is very important to the ascension of the country, one that has no chance of being voted down, that a partisan rider has a good chance of being approved. This is a very disgraceful way of doing business, but it speaks volumes about the character of the people who utilize this tactic.

People "In Charge"

The problem is that people "in charge" feel like they are most important when the opposite is true. The leaders of our country are responsible for the well-being of the people, not themselves. Rarely do you see any self-sacrifice. Their actions usually seem selfless on the surface, but it usually serves them in some way. It's also disconcerting when people say "we the people" are in charge yet do nothing to ensure that is true. They keep electing the same selfish people to office and continue to suffer. If the people of this country truly wanted change, they wouldn't complain that there should be term limits, they would simply vote the current people out of office every 2-3 terms, or sooner if necessary.

People in charge (all people in charge, not just elected officials) should feel lucky they are in their positions. When I held leadership positions, I always felt humbled by the opportunity and responsibility and tried my hardest to ensure those "under" me had everything they needed. This was especially important in my line because those people were going to war and if they didn't get what they needed it could result in their injury or death. I never respected leaders who walked around like they owned the place and did things simply because they could.

The President

The president is the ultimate public servant. I always found it odd that we treat that position with such reverence when it is a completely elected office that's only prerequisites are that the candidate is a natural born U.S. citizen, has resided in the U.S. for 14 years, and is at least 35 years old. That's it. They are not gods or superheroes, they are simply the person that one of the two major parties decided they wanted as their candidate and then half of the people thought would be a good leader. The president is the least important person in the country, yet we treat him like the most. We guard him as if his absence will somehow result in the country crumbling down. It wouldn't and it won't, we have protocols in place for just such an incident. That's why those in succession for the president are briefed on most, if not all, of what's important (or they should be). The notion that if something happens to the president our nation will weaken is antiquated.

Bureaucracy

People wonder why the government takes so long to accomplish anything, it's called bureaucracy and it is a cancer that no one seems to want to remove. Our leaders are more concerned with how they look and growing their bank account than they are with taking care of the people. I truly believe our Founding Fathers, with all their faults truly cared about the people and the country. The same is not true, and hasn't been for some time, for modern day politicians. They are mostly actors who attempt to replicate politicians' actions before them instead of being themselves. It's painfully obvious how politicians today try so hard to look like politicians instead of simply stating facts, being honest, and actually helping the country. They speak in ambiguities, talking points, and BS. There have been a few lately who have attempted to be genuine but they always fall back into the status quo so their peers take them seriously, as if this is more important than earning the people's respect. When a politician gets behind a microphone they immediately go into fake mode and spew their garbage. But there's a reason why most politicians speak this way, because they are unable to speak any other way and make any sense. Our elected officials are portrayed as if they were anointed sometimes but people fail to realize that politicians are ELECTED, not ordained. They are people, just like us, who convinced their districts to vote for them. Most of the ones I've seen can't even speak with a teleprompter, let alone off the cuff. We need to be more selective in this country or we will continue to get treated the same way we always have. People hate Trump for who he is, how he speaks, and from where he came but the fact that he does what he said he was going to do is indisputable. We just need to find a likeable person who does what's best for the country to unify us. If only all politicians did what they said they would do for us, but they can't because what they promised are lies and impossible to accomplish. The people of this country need to wake up and simply vote people out who have not done what they said they would do. Check their records, hold them accountable.

Frivolous Hearings

How do we let our elected officials get away with holding time, money, and effort wasting investigations and hearings? They have little to no hard evidence, yet they conduct long, drawn out trials that go nowhere or call-in celebrities to testify about nothing and nothing comes of it. I think the elected officials should be fined if it is found that they have been disingenuous when presenting a weak, or non-existent, case for political reasons. It's obvious to everyone but them that their efforts are futile, yet they go forward with the proceedings to showboat and get on TV.

Getting Things Done

Why is it so hard for elected officials to get anything done? For instance, how many times has our own congress been a majority of the same party as the president? Enough to make change, yet they still can't get it done. Why? It's as if they don't want to, maybe to keep the status quo? Maybe they draw things out to give the illusion that they're actually "working"? Maybe they don't care, as long as their investments are doing well (or however else an upper middle-class person reaches millionaire status in a government job). There are a considerable number of problems that seem to have easy fixes or easy beginnings with a lot of work after, yet government works so slowly and inefficiently. Issues necessary for the wellbeing of the nation take an exorbitant amount of time to come to fruition, if at all. It's a "secret" society of which only the members really know the rules and goings on. Why don't the so called "crusaders" within the government drop dime on the others? Are they scared? Lack of evidence? Lazy? It's a mystery. There are books documenting what happens when a person is elected to congress and how shady it is, but they don't seem to have made a difference. The only true way to ensure that change occurs is to make it. Voters can impose term limits with their votes but, that would require us all to agree, and we know how well that always works. Instead, the same old people keep getting elected and doing nothing besides grandstanding and toeing party lines to make it look like they're doing something so their rich constituents can feel good about themselves. It's amazing how multi-billion-dollar companies can fix problems and grow yet our own government can't figure it out. Perhaps there should be more businessmen and less lawyers in power?

In the military, if you need to rewrite a regulation or standard operating procedure you appoint someone, a point of contact or POC, to either draft one if it doesn't exist or modify the existing one. Then, that POC disseminates the document to those who should have inputs on it along with a "suspense" (time limit for comments/inputs) to get it back to the POC. Once the POC gathers all inputs they incorporate those inputs into the draft for approval by the boss. The boss will make his/her edits and then call a meeting with his/her staff to finalize the document. The document is then signed, and everyone is expected to adhere to it. Why can't the government do this? I touched on a bill earlier but, to reiterate, instead of having a bill start in the house (with only a select few people on a committee by the way), and then go to the senate for concurrence, and then to the president for approval, why not get all those entities in the same room (in person or virtually). Once assembled, they can then discuss all the issues that would prevent the bill from becoming law and continue to meet until the bill becomes law. Government officials are our employees, they should answer to us and should be held accountable when they don't perform their job. Unfortunately, like I said, that would require most of us to agree and that seems like a pipe dream. So, we have the system we have, one that first and foremost benefits those in power and may never benefit all the people it claims to represent. Why don't they follow the same laws as us citizens? It seems like a very simple solution. The problem with this is that it could be easy, but those in power choose to make it hard because they don't have your (the people) best interests at heart.

Picking a candidate

It seems that people gravitate toward a certain type of candidate based on generic views or outlooks on life, but I don't do it that way. I've never had any loyalty to a particular party because both parties are the same and contain the same kinds of people. Now, when I say "party", I'm not talking about all the members but the leadership and candidates. For the most part they are all politicians and only serve themselves. That's what made Trump so different, he couldn't care less about a party, he actually said so on video when he said if he ran for president he would run as a republican because they are easily fooled. I don't think he necessarily "fooled" everyone, he was simply the last candidate left standing, mainly because the other candidates were weak and couldn't stand toe to toe with him. If there was a strong candidate who made sense and could trade jabs with Trump, he probably would have won the nomination and possibly the presidency. Unfortunately, the people who could challenge Trump don't run for office.

As I said, I don't have any loyalty to any particular party, I look at the candidate as a person and evaluate their positions on issues that affect this country. This seems like the most logical conclusion, but our country doesn't work that way. Most people either vote all republican or all democrat because it's easier. Some are under the impression that their party's candidates have their best interest in mind, or they stand to benefit from their party's candidates getting elected. Elections have very little to do with the individual (as illustrated with the left's support of Biden). Yes, some candidates appear to care and appear to be "different", but they quickly conform to the system, mainly out of survival, but also because they, deep down, are politicians and that's what politicians do, take care of themselves first. I don't think we need anymore "career politicians" in our government. I think we need people who are smart in the ways of government but are true public servants who are focused on the job of actually helping people instead of making themselves rich. It can't be an issue of compensation since most politicians gain wealth in office. It probably has more to do with the hassle of running for office and the scrutiny that befalls candidates.

Most people who would do a great job serving others don't want their lives upended. Politicians seem to welcome it or at least not mind it. It should be illegal to "expose" a candidate when you don't have clear cut evidence of the accusation against a person. Just mentioning something that MAY have happened in the candidate's past can ruin them. Once it's out there, people immediately believe it and by the time the actual truth comes out the candidate has endured massive amounts of accusations and detestation that it's almost impossible to bounce back. The story should be airtight before it can surface and, if the story is disproven then the originators, and all who proliferated the lie, should be held accountable.

Abolish Political Parties

There shouldn't be parties, they should be outlawed because they limit the choices during an election. How can two non-governmental organizations have so much power over our government? How did we let this happen? How do we as a society let these two corrupt organizations manipulate us by only allowing us to choose between two people?

We don't actually have to let them choose for us. There are laws and stipulations that allow for others to be on the ballot, but we fear the "third party" vote because we feel it's a vote for the other side. This is lunacy, especially for the party who obviously has a weak candidate. Why do they let their "party" decide for them? The craziest example is happening as I write this, 77-year-old Joe Biden is the democrat presidential candidate. The party that is supposed to be representing anyone other than old, straight, white males has an old, straight, white male as their candidate. They had homosexuals, women, and dark-skinned people vying for the presidency and they disregarded all of them to select the guy who looks most like their idea of their opponent. It really makes you wonder what exactly is going on with the presidential election. How does Joe Biden represent the democrat base? It's crazy. Yet, he's the candidate and now everyone on the left has to back him. Like I said, they don't have to, they can start a grassroots campaign for someone else and simply write that person in. But this will never happen because that would entail people coming together and, again, we know how that usually works out.

Campaign Finance

There should be a cap on campaign finance as well. Each candidate should have a cap on how much they can raise and how much they can spend. This would level the playing field and allow those who don't have much money to stay in the race. The amount of money raised usually has very little to do with how good the candidate is. People who can buy the most ad time, etc. shouldn't be the only choices for us.

Speaking of campaign finance reform, my daughter had a good idea: when raising campaign finances, make it mandatory that a portion must be used to help the country in some way. Force the candidates to put their money where their mouth is by choosing a program that helps the people the candidate means to lead. In that same vein, my daughter asked why the government can't simply ask for money from our wealthier citizens, the "1%". It's not a bad idea, simply present a program that helps U.S. citizens and ask wealthy citizens and corporations to fund, and run, it. The private sector has long proven its ability to successfully manage programs the government consistently fails to. I realize this last part has nothing to do with campaign finance but maybe limiting funds from wealthy donors will focus their efforts on more philanthropic issues?

CONGRESS

The most frustrating thing about our government is that the legislative branch has the power to do everything necessary to "fix" the nation, yet they screw it up more often than not. This is mainly due to partisan politics getting in the way of common-sense legislation. Their decisions are based on party politics not the needs of the people. Take the spending bills, for instance. They are chock full of funding for people, unfortunately, not all of those people are Americans.

𝕭ills and 𝕽esolutions

I've talked about bills and how they are too convoluted, confusing, and bloated for most Americans to read, let alone understand. The most recent spending resolution congress is attempting to pass at the time of this writing is over five thousand pages and has millions of dollars going to foreign countries. Shouldn't we help out the less fortunate? Sure, but maybe we should help our own people first? I mean, what does it say when American children are starving but our legislative branch thinks Pakistani gender programs are more important.

Bills and resolutions should be limited in size and scope. The Constitution was four pages. All other bills should follow this example. They should be short and simple enough for the average American to read and understand and contain one issue each. As it stands, even the members of congress don't have enough time to read the resolutions before they vote on them. Countless senators and representatives openly admitted to not reading H.R. 133 before voting on it.

Unfortunately, the reason these bills and resolutions are so long is that they are touted as one thing (COVID-19 relief) yet contain several different issues, expenses, and/or proposals hidden within them. Instead, congress should present each one of these issues separately so Americans can see exactly what congress has planned for our tax dollars. I believe this is by design so We The People don't notice items that were included in the, so-called, COVID-19 Relief Bill, such as the $100m to Sudan or the $1B to the Smithsonian, or provisions for horseracing and NASCAR. Here's the link to the resolution if you want to see it for yourself:

https://www.congress.gov/bill/116th-congress/house-bill/133.

We also need to stop letting those who "predict" what will happen stop common sense legislation. I too often hear about entities like the Congressional Budget Office advising against legislation based on costs not benefit to the people.

The military has been hamstrung by this way of thinking for some time, bowing to the bean counters while warfighter training suffers. Our government wastes billions a year, how does the CBO determine on which initiatives to waste money? I'm sure it's way over my head but I do know that no one can predict the future and I also know that saving money isn't always the most important goal, especially when it comes to helping the people of this country. It's not like the government has a stellar track record with being good stewards of The People's money, I think The People would be ok with spending a great deal of money if it helped them in the long run.

Two Party System

How have "we the people" allowed the two-party system to exist as long as it has? Two PRIVATE organizations have absolute control over our country. Can no one see that their only goal is to win and gain/keep power? They have no interest in the people of this country, only manipulating the people for their own gain and to keep people they can control in office. How is it possible that our government officials are defined by a private corporation's designation? No one working in our government should be shackled to any private organization, let alone be defined by them, yet each congressperson either has a D or an R next to their name. It seems very inappropriate. Do people really think their loyalties lie with the state they represent? They would never defy the party because they need them too much to get reelected which, after all, is their ultimate goal.

What about the hypocrisy? I love it when people say, "do they think we're that stupid?" and the answer is yes, they do, that's why they continue to do it and, to a certain extent, we are because we keep voting for the same offenders. They complain about the horrible behavior of their rival and then later do the exact same thing. It's lunacy. So, in a way, we are too stupid to do anything about it because "we" keep electing the same people. Who are these people, you say? They are the same people who receive millions of dollars from people who want them to do their bidding. It definitely isn't the people but, unfortunately, the people vote for who they are told will represent them the best, even though that candidate has failed to do that very thing for decades! Are they just waiting for the politician to come through on their promise? Are they just giving them another chance, each time hoping the politician makes good on their promises? Or do they blame the other side? "Well, if the other side would have worked with my candidate, they would have kept their promises!" Which is the point, these "public servants" do whatever it takes to stay in office except the one thing we the people need them to do which is look out for us. The solution? Vote all the incumbents out of office. Clean the slate. Vote in new blood. Vote for people that are hungry for justice and not corrupted by the system (yet). Too often we hear these old politicians talk down to us "ignorant" masses because we don't know how "the system" works and we should just trust that they know what's best, and we do!

The "system" does work very well, unfortunately it doesn't work for us. "We" sit idly by while the Pelosis, and McConnells, and Schumers, and Grahams stay in power and look out for their own interests and conduct pseudo-battles against the other side in an attempt to fool us rubes who don't know any better. Don't wait for them to vote on things like term limits, we the people can impose our own term limits with our vote. There are more of us regular citizens than there are billionaires and corporations. We just have to do it.

It really is frustrating that the same people who make the laws either don't have to abide by them or create laws from which only they benefit. Working in one of the three branches of our government should be absolutely exhausting and thankless – it's the only way to guarantee that the person being elected has nothing but the American people's best interests in mind. Take away the reasons that a corrupt person seeks office, and they will cease to do so. Our government officials shouldn't want subsequent terms – it should be that hard.

Insurrection

In January of 2021, a group of idiots "stormed" the capitol and forced "the People's business" to be delayed. Everyone was up in arms about this act because of the meaning they placed upon it. Were they trying to take over the government? If so, why were they escorted by Capitol Police or, at least not being engaged by them? (https://www.youtube.com/watch?v=xfZHk1zu6Vw) Yes, the Capitol Police were outmanned and probably outgunned but why didn't they call for reinforcements? Yes, the five deaths were an absolute tragedy (four of which were protestors, and one who died of natural causes), but for anyone to call this anything other than a slight delay in "the People's business" is being willfully ignorant and overtly disingenuous. Not to mention that there is proof of at least one "left wing" agitator (https://www.politico.com/news/2021/01/14/liberal-activist-charged-capitol-riot-459553) in the midst of the "Trump supporters". It only takes one idiot to instigate something like this, and they did. My point is that people are making more about this than it really is. Congress reconvened later that day after no armed response as most of the suspects not only left on their own, but the crowd dispersed to honor the curfew implemented by the government.

What's my point? More people are upset about an "insurrection" that lasted a couple of hours than they are with our own government attempting to overthrow our own government on a daily basis. Yes, the most recent example of this is Democrats relentlessly pursuing impeachment from the first day of President Trump's term but that isn't the only example of it. Neither side is innocent, they both intentionally sabotage, filibuster, and outright block progress if they think it benefits the other side. Every president has to endure the self-righteous crusaders on the opposite side, "fighting for the people", as if we don't know they're full of it and only doing it to be pugnacious.

Yes, the "rules" they make are perfectly "legal" but only because the same "insurrectionists" vote on the ridiculous rules they make for themselves. This is why they keep getting raises and not term limits. Think how much farther our country would have progressed if the people in Congress actually worked toward a common ground instead of constantly trying to stop each other. This constant blockage of the People's business is exponentially more detrimental than the interruption on January 6th. Anyone who thinks differently is being overly dramatic, which I attribute to this generation wanting so much to be historic that they blow every situation out of proportion to ensure it is solidified in history. What would people do if there was an actual insurrection? They would lose their minds.

Now, do I think what those protestors did was wrong? Of course, it was just as stupid as any other protest. I don't differentiate between protest and riot because neither of them are protected by the First Amendment. As usual, people have twisted the terminology to suit their wants. This is what it says, *"peaceably to assemble, and to petition the Government for a redress of grievances"*. This doesn't mean holding disparaging signs, or yelling, etc. It means to gather and petition the GOVERNMENT for a redress of grievances. If anything, most of the "rioters" on January 6th were actually exercising this right. They were actually petitioning the government, not looting, burning property, or beating people almost to death. To clarify, the ones that did damage or hurt people were the same as any other thug, but I saw a great deal of people holding flags, walking calmly, and praying. Did they go about it the wrong way? Yes. Were they goaded into entering the Capitol by agitators? There's at least one instance where that happened. But for the most part they were saying prayers, laughing, and taking selfies with cops. Conversely, most of the other protests we've seen in recent years do not come close to the definition in the Constitution. I don't think MLK Jr. would have approved of most of the protests that have occurred in recent years.

How do we the people allow our government to spend so much? It's really not even most people in congress, it's mostly just those who have been in there a long time and have manipulated the system to work in their favor and keep the status quo, and blame the other party for the debt, deficit, etc. In reality, it's all their fault because they alone have the power to fix it. We the people can only vote them in and out, once they're in there they do whatever they want because it serves those who got them elected, the rich and their political party (which are pretty much synonymous). It really has gotten terrible. These "public servants" get on tv or on the floor of the house/senate and spew their BS and grandstand about the injustices of their political opponents, yet nothing changes. But, as I said, it's our fault because we have the power to vote them out, but we don't. We let them stay where they are and let them continue to make our country weak while China, and other competitors, grow strong. I don't think it's a sinister plan (although it seems that way sometimes, and may be for some, to an extent) but simple laziness, greed, and complacency. They either act, or genuinely feel, that they're serving us, but they aren't. If they truly were "servants of the people", more things would get done, but just like any other government agency, congress is rife with do nothings and narcissists.

The People's Best Interests

If there was any question about whether the current congress had "our" best interests at heart, just observe their actions when they control the House, Senate, and White House. For instance, both Obama and Trump enjoyed a unified government during their first terms, but did they do anything significant with that power? Not that I could tell. If you genuinely cared about "the people" I would think you would work day and night to affect change and help as much as possible before you lost unification. Unfortunately, our congress is only worried about reelection, gaining/keeping power, and making money - helping the people of this nation often (always) gets in the way of that.

The truth is, they only care about what will make them look good and therefore acquire them votes. There are far too many issues for our "leaders" to deal with and still focus on their campaign, stock portfolio, television appearances, etc. Instead, they "champion" a cause or two and create the façade that they are actually working for the people. How crazy is it that our "lawmakers" help us so seldomly that when they actually do something for us, they celebrate and grandstand on tv, and tell you how much they have helped you. It's literally their job to help us and they act like they're doing us a favor.

This is blatantly obvious with regard to finances and investments. They tell you to be patient and let the market correct when they govern improperly but I say they should be held accountable when their decisions result in the plight of the American people. It is our "leaders'" sole purpose to ensure the people of this country are afforded every opportunity to excel. At the very least they are not supposed to be a roadblock to our ascension and, when they are, they should make it up to us.

Vote Exposure

Too often, the legislators of this country do an absolutely unforgiveable thing, they vote "present" or refuse to vote at all. This is unacceptable. The lawmakers of this country have one job and that is to make the laws of this country. There shouldn't be an option not to vote or to simply vote "present" and not take a side. This is a dereliction of duty and should be punished.

Speaking of "the vote", any time there is a vote in the house or senate, it should not only be televised but it should preempt all television shows like they used to do when the president spoke. The passing of these laws is integral to the operation of this country and affects us all. We should have a "front row" seat for every decision being made by our public servants. Additionally, as I've said, the bills on which they vote should be one subject each and be worded in simple terms the average American can understand. Another reason for the televised vote is to see who actually voted and how.

This will ensure the "representatives" of our respective districts and states are voting with our best interests in mind instead of with their cowardice or bank account.

Troop Levels

I find it odd that the legislative branch of our government is in charge of troop levels when they have no idea of the actual requirements. The military units of our country are perpetually undermanned and overworked in order to save money for projects that either don't work very well or never come to fruition. Meanwhile, the men and women of our military are doing more with less, and often less with less, and never have a chance to really do their job well because they are too stressed over doing the job of two or three people.

Congress needs to reevaluate how they do things to ensure the proper number of people are employed. I've been around the military my whole life and I have seen this firsthand. Granted, not everyone works hard but the ones whose jobs aren't very arduous still have important jobs in the military. Then, on the other hand, there are those military members, and DOD civilians, who do the work of two or three people. This imbalance is bad for morale and bad for the people who are burdened with this overwork.

It's always been the mentality of the military to keep your nose to the grindstone, don't complain, and especially don't let the chain of command know that you need help. Too often unit commanders will report that their unit is "full up" and that they don't need any more help to do the mission because that looks bad on them. They habitually file false "wellness" reports, either by choice or because of their ignorance, and it results in the suffering of their subordinates.

The bottom line is that Congress needs to do a better job of investigating what the military actually needs instead of simply relying on generals to inform them. Generals very rarely ever know what's happening at the lower levels because any time a general visits a subordinate unit, the commander of that unit ensures the place looks nothing like it does on a daily basis. The place is deep cleaned, all the "issues" with the unit are hidden, and only "big ticket" items are discussed with the general as to "not waste the general's time with minutiae". Unfortunately, no one understands that troop morale, overwork, and dwindling budgets are not minutiae but the foundation on which a unit is built and are necessary for unit success.

Regrettably, in an attempt to overcorrect, and fall in line with the "woke" society in which we live, those in power have ensured that social issues have come to the forefront and now overshadow the real issues I mentioned earlier. Instead of identifying, and solving, real problems that have a direct effect on the mission, those "in charge" have created more "offices" and more work for those already overworked members to "solve" a non-issue or, an issue for which there are already regulations in place to solve.

𝕷𝖎𝖛𝖎𝖓𝖌 𝖎𝖓 𝖆 𝖁𝖆𝖈𝖚𝖚𝖒

Speaking of Congress being ignorant to "real problems", I often ask myself how politicians can be so incredibly dishonest and disingenuous, but the answer is obvious. They are surrounded by people like them, who buy into the D.C. BS and perpetuate the garbage because no one is being honest with them about how lame they are. Or they know but they feel like the American people, and the world, are so incredibly stupid that we won't catch on to their insincerity.

I truly believe that they feel righteous when they get on tv or hold a rally and speak to us like we're children. Like they are our saviors or benevolent leaders, and not the servants they actually are. It really is crazy how incredibly lame everyone thinks they are and how incredibly awesome they think they are. Again, no one is telling them anything differently, and they wouldn't acknowledge it if anyone did because they feel they're right. They feel like they know more than everyone else simply based on the number of votes they received in an election. I've said it many times before, we need to start holding these people accountable. If they don't perform, then they need to be voted out of office. But people say that if we vote them all out then our government will seize but that's not true. Congress, much like the president, are simply figure heads who manage those beneath them. It's ludicrous to think that losing politicians will somehow stop the government.

Although, government shutdowns happen once in a while and the country doesn't seem to notice. Granted, those who work in government are affected, but for the majority of Americans who don't, they seem to bode very well. It's as if a smaller, less intrusive government is the answer to our problems.

Until we stop paying attention to politicians' bloviating and start holding them accountable, we'll never truly have righteous people run for office. They're stuck in their vacuum with little to no touch with the true outside world. Yes, they speak to influential people in their district/state to see which way they need to vote, and which stocks to pick, but it seems that they couldn't care less about "regular" people and what they truly need to succeed. I guess it's because we're only here on this planet for a short time and most people are only interested in their own way of life and will do whatever it takes to preserve it and taking care of the little guy isn't lucrative. Instead, they speak in abstracts and make bold, broad-brush claims that are unquantifiable and never really go anywhere. They also try too hard to nitpick the "other side" instead of showing everyone what good they can do for the country. In the previous sentence I put "other side" in quotes because they aren't really the "other side" but the second half of a whole. We all know they all collaborate and conspire with each other but never show it to us because usually their collaborations and conspirations have little or nothing to do with our well-being. They covertly set the deck to ensure they are prosperous while overtly "hating" the other side to keep all of us fighting each other instead of banding together to challenge them. It's textbook population control and it's fairly easy to do when people aren't paying attention. Then again, like I said, we're only here a short time so not many people pay the attention required to keep our "leaders" in check, which is how our "leaders" want it.

𝕌nnecessary Complexity

When discussing the "lawmakers" of this country, our forefathers intentionally made our governing documents simple and unambiguous so the people of this country could understand the laws that govern this land. Unfortunately, because of their megalomaniacal successors, the laws currently on our books are extremely large and complicated.

Now, we all know this is by design to ensure that We The People either can't, or don't have time to, read and understand the laws, heck, even most of the lawmakers don't know what's in the bills they vote into law. Remember when a House member said we have to pass the bill first to know what's in it?

This is how those in power push their agendas and become millionaires while in public service. They jam through legislation that benefits only a few, if any, of the citizens in this country while the rest of us are left to pay for it all. They swear they won't raise taxes and then absolutely do without any hint of remorse or embarrassment. This is also by design. They know that they can say and do whatever they want because no one, at least no significant amount, is paying attention. Lawmakers are free to act in their own best interests as long as they say what people want to hear.

It really is crazy that "everyone" seems to know this, yet no one does anything about it. I speak to people who complain about certain issues their party is doing to them yet consistently vote "all blue" or "all red". First of all, there shouldn't be "red" or "blue" choices, there should simply be people who do not pledge any allegiances to political parties, but to ALL the people of this country. This would force people to actually research the candidates to ensure they are voting for people who are truly willing to help. Instead, they complain about taxes and overspending and then vote democrat, or they complain about "unlawful" wars or taking care of Americans before providing aid to other countries, and then vote republican. It makes no sense. Well, it makes some sense. Americans never want to stick their neck out and be the first one to vote for someone other than the democrat or republican. They think they'll waste their vote if they don't support "their party". Just think if everyone voted for the people they think would do the best job instead of the person most supported by each of the parties.

Back to unnecessary complexity. In the military we used to say, "keep it simple" – actually we said keep it simple, stupid, I guess because then they could use the acronym KISS but I stayed away from the stupid part and just said "keep it simple".

Everything can be simplified, boiled down, and streamlined. Answers can be found, workable solutions can be implemented, and real results can be achieved by keeping it simple. However, like I said, no one in Washington is interested in keeping it simple. They would rather it be convoluted and ambiguous to allow for different interpretations, thereby giving them leeway to do whatever they want. It also serves the purpose of saying a lot without having any definitive directives or the potential to garner quantifiable results. Often the results are the opposite of what was told to us with either a weak excuse (wasn't our fault) or no explanation at all because usually it is forgotten by most, if it was ever realized at all. If I were president, I wouldn't sign anything that wasn't simple, concise, and didn't have measurable results.

PRESIDENTIAL GOALS

Service

Speaking of service, my entire life has been about service. From a career in the military to working for child protection in Alaska to working as a contractor for the U.S. Government, all my jobs have been in the service of others. Include my work as a Girl Scout Leader, swim and soccer coach, youth group leader, and school chaperone and you can see that serving others has been a large part of my life. Most of the time I was either in a position to help and did so or was specifically asked and I accepted. I think more things would get done if more people did the same thing. Being presented with an opportunity, or specifically asked to help, is much easier than seeking out volunteer or service opportunities. If more people took advantage of these situations, I believe our world would be better for everyone.

As you can see, I'm not a politician, I'm a servant of the people and through that lens, as President, I'll view all the issues that come across my desk. The presidency, and any other elected position, should be so absolutely exhausting that incumbents wouldn't want another term. They should be so spent from serving the people who elected them that they have no other choice but to not seek reelection.

Objectives

1. Due to the Covid-19 outbreak, we have proven that the government can conduct business remotely or not at all. Think how much money this can save. This pandemic has proven just how insignificant most government agencies are. There are those who are not benefitting from teleworking or unable to and they should certainly be able to work with precautions in place. Hopefully by the time you read this we have a vaccine, but we have proven that the government can operate in this situation with considerably less people going into work.

2. I don't think there should be a tax on winning. Whether it be at the casino, lottery, a game show, etc. Why should you have to pay the government for something you won? It makes no sense. I do, however, think there should be an exorbitant tax on "decision"

items, things you make a choice to purchase, but don't necessarily need. Things that don't really serve any other purpose other than to "entertain". Food, clothing, shelter (primary shelter, not a summer home) shouldn't be taxed at all. We need these items to survive, why are we penalized for buying them? If someone chooses to buy something they don't "need" (based on the bottom three levels of Maslow's Hierarchy of Needs) then they should pay tax on it.

3. Another way we can save this country money is to go to a four day/thirty-two-hour work week. If not for everyone then just government agencies. Believe me, government employees waste a lot of time at work. Why not give them more time with their families and decrease their stress levels? Not only that but stagger the times people come in and leave each day. It's

ludicrous that we make every single government employee come in at the same time, causing unnecessary gridlock. Then they all take lunch at the same time, resulting in more traffic and huge lines at the same restaurants everyone uses due to their distance from work. Then we make them all leave at the same time creating an even bigger traffic jam. People spend way too much time in their cars getting from home to work and back again. This is lunacy that can be stopped. There is no need, as proven with all the Covid-19 teleworking, to have everyone in person, at their desk, at the same time. If you need someone, call them. If there is a meeting, telecom. If someone must sign something, have them sign it electronically. There will be times when everyone is at work at the same time and can have the "vital" in person meeting, but we all know what a waste of time most meetings are so why not just send an email or conduct a video teleconference? If it requires discussion, telecom. If only some of the people are there, have them meet and the rest telecom. For most people, a secure telecom is only necessary occasionally. When it is, make sure everyone knows and they can all show up in person. Some will scoff at this proposition but only because they can't envision it. They have been stuck in this 40 hour/5-day work week rut for so long that they can't imagine anything else. I can't believe people haven't demanded more time off. We go in on Monday and "work" for 5 days and then get two days off? It's not even two days really. On Sunday you must mentally prepare for Monday, so you really only have Saturday to yourself. We spend most of our lives at work and most people probably aren't working a full 40 hours anyway. Why not give them an extra day so they're not burnt out by Friday? There are those who love to be at work and to them I say "great! Work from home or go in to work and "get some stuff done" but I don't think it's necessary. Government "production" can't get any worse so why not give people an extra day to live their lives? I know what the government will say: "we're paying you to be here, so you need to be here" which is the craziest thing I've ever heard. They're paying people to be in a building, at a desk, in the hopes that they'll be productive but, from what I've experienced, that seldom happens.

Some might say that people rely on government agencies to be there for them and to that I say, hire more workers and instill split schedules. Some people could work Monday through Thursday while others work Tuesday through Friday. Another way to alleviate this issue is to move everything online. Forego the necessity to speak to someone or visit an actual office. Take Estonia, for instance. The only thing you can't do online in Estonia is get married, divorced, and conduct real estate transactions. Everything else is done online. This would allow most government workers to assist customers from anywhere (if necessary), allow people

24/7 access to their information, and significantly decrease operating costs.

4. Speaking of "government", I've been using that word like it's an entity in and of itself, but the government is made of many different people, who all have differing views of how employees should behave. Some couldn't care less about the clock; others care too much and watch the clock like the government is going to shut down if a person is 5 minutes late. Then there are those who lead their people in a way that empowers them and enables them to be self-starters (and finishers), ensuring that they feel valued which leads to them wanting to be there and wanting to work. When I was in the military, and lead troops, I couldn't have cared less what time they got to work or what time they left as long as things got done. If it took them shorter than the "duty day" to get the work done, they would cut out early and if the job required more of the "duty day" they would stay longer. Our government has never, really,

been "results" driven, only time driven, which is odd given that an entity is successful based on their accomplishments, not their time in the building. I've seen some government employees do absolutely nothing all day long yet brag about how they were in before everyone and left after everyone. "I put in my time" they'd say but had nothing to show for it and contributed zilch to the progress of the country. Very weird thing to brag about, being on time, when that's not the goal. Now, if there is a meeting where people are waiting on you, show up on time. If you must do something at a specific time, be there 15 minutes early. But if your job is results oriented, not time oriented, why is it important when you get there and when you leave? I've had jobs where I was the last one in and the first one out and I did PT while I was there and took a lunch break and still did exponentially more than most of the people in the office. It's about results and actual work. Which is why a 32 hour/4-day work week is a good idea, it gives people more of a break so they might be more productive when they are at work, not to mention it saves on electricity, water, etc.

5. We also need more Federal holidays. At least one per month on a Thursday with a "family" day on the following Monday and, since we are now operating under a 4 day/32-hour work week, it will result in a five-day weekend each month. Most people are wasting their lives at work, and I believe that they would be more productive if they received more time off.

6. I would give federal grants for school security, to include, but not limited to, resource officers, security systems, and metal detectors. It'll be part of the education budget and be mandatory. You want to prevent school shootings, defend against them.

7. I would provide funding to law enforcement agencies but, in order to get the money, they must pass physical fitness, mobility (tactical driving, accident avoidance, etc.), medical, and marksmanship tests. If a department doesn't have enough officers to allow them to train on these tasks during work hours, then the numbers of officers must be increased. This may seem unrealistic but not compared to the billions of dollars wasted on programs that do not benefit the nation. The funding will be used to hire more officers to allow for training during work hours and to hire experts to train officers on the aforementioned tasks. Another option is to form a federal agency that trains police departments across the U.S. This agency would be comprised of experts in the skills mentioned above. In addition to these tasks, LEOs would be given periodic psych evaluations and receive monthly, if not weekly, training in negotiation techniques. Every LEO should be an expert in the four basic tasks but also have the

mental training to only need those skills once negotiations have failed.

Government Social Programs

There has been much controversy and discussion about the implications of allowing people to procreate at will. On the one hand, people are free to have as many children as they want but they are also responsible for those children. However, in this country, we incentivize having children, an unfortunate byproduct of helping people. The government saw that people, mostly single mothers, were struggling to take care of their children so they reached out to help but, in doing so, they made it very lucrative to keep having children – the very definition of a vicious cycle. Objectives continued:

8. There should be a cap on how many children a family can claim to receive government funds. If you continue to have children knowing that you cannot support them then you are being irresponsible and

should not be rewarded for such behavior. There must be stipulations for people who receive "government help" (which is just another way of saying "taxpayer money"). It is unfair for those who pay taxes and do not receive government help to pay for those who are irresponsible and live outside their means. I realize that there are circumstances outside a person's control like a breadwinning spouse leaving or dying, etc. but I don't believe this is always the case and each case should be evaluated to ensure the legitimacy of the claim. Also, once the legitimacy of the claim is established, there needs to be a plan implemented to wean the recipient off government assistance so they can operate on their own. There must also be drug testing and frequent visits to check receipts to ensure the money is being spent appropriately. The idea of simply giving out money to people who have already been irresponsible or are "gaming" the system is ludicrous. Again, I realize that not everyone is doing this but, unfortunately, those who are make it hard for everyone. The government, in order to be good stewards of the people's money, must scrutinize every beneficiary to ensure they are not trying to defraud the government and steal taxpayer money.

9. This model also applies to those who seek health care from the government. People are demanding free universal health care paid for by those who pay for their own health care and pay taxes that would cover this "free" health care for all. Usually those who demand free health care don't pay taxes at all anyway so it's a "win" for them. I'm not against helping people with their health care and, while it shouldn't be "free", it should be attainable. If the government was in the health care business for all people, there should be stipulations like the beneficiary must exercise, and eat correctly, not smoke or do drugs, etc. This would

lower the chances of people needing health care and keep the cost low. If we simply gave out free healthcare but didn't insist on people living healthy lifestyles, the program would be unsustainable (not that it wouldn't be anyway given the government's track record on running things.) Again, if you are requesting assistance from an entity, whoever they are, it is not unreasonable to follow their rules to receive that assistance. If people feel these stipulations are unfair, then they should provide for themselves and free themselves of any outside control.

State's Rights and Responsibilities

U.S. States should have the freedom to govern themselves if the laws do not affect other states, and for the most part they do. Each state in the union is so unique it is impossible to have a "one size fits all" model for all states. The federal government should be limited to border security, foreign affairs, interstate travel and commerce, etc. The federal government should only be involved if the issue affects all states equally. I think the federal government has far too much overreach and doesn't allow the states to freely operate how they want. I also think that we should reform the financial aid each state receives from the federal government. The focus of the federal government should be balancing the budget, getting rid of the debt, and rebuilding/improving infrastructure. This country was founded on hard work and dedication, our leaders should have that same focus. I believe the states should be allowed to thrive or fail as they deserve. If the governments of failing states aren't doing their job correctly then the people need to vote them out of office. It is not the federal government's job to bail out those who choose not to help themselves. People need to stop feeling helpless against their government and start taking a proactive position against those who do not act accordingly. It only takes a short internet search to find out your elected official's voting record and, if they are not voting correctly according to what your state wants, then vote them out of office, the same should be done for state legislatures. The people hold the true power, but they simply won't wield it. They vote with fear, or tradition, or based on lies they've been told. We need to come together as one community, set our differences aside, and control the government with our votes to prevent the government from controlling us.

Federal Budget

We need to hold our government accountable for not balancing the budget. It's unacceptable for us to expect people to pay their taxes, etc., when the government can't even "live" within their means. A complete review and revamping of the federal budget must be accomplished. The COVID-19 pandemic illustrated just how much money we waste and how few agencies/employees we need to operate the country. The problem is that the proper time and effort is not being applied to this endeavor therefore it will always be an issue. The government needs to revisit all outgoing payments to determine their validity. If it does not directly contribute to the betterment of the U.S. and its citizens, it should be stopped. The government is not a good steward of the people's money, as illustrated by all the frivolous senate hearings and congressional inquiries that occur.

Our country also needs to find more revenue streams. We need to collect debts owed to us, and we could also do things like hold a nationwide lottery or legalize gambling in all states. Whatever we decide it must be implemented because taxing our people to cover everything doesn't seem to be working. Currently, we only receive 5% of our income from "other" sources. The rest is in some form of tax and most of it is income tax, a tax that 44% of the people in the nation don't pay. This is unacceptable. Everyone should pay something. If this occurred then everyone, theoretically, could pay less. The only "fair" way to tax people is to make everyone pay the same percentage. This seems very simple and effective, but I don't think the government is concerned with simplicity and they obviously aren't concerned at all with effectiveness. If our elected officials were as concerned with improving this country as they were with getting reelected, we would be in much better shape. The amount of money that is wasted by our government each year is unimaginable, think about how many people could be helped if the budget was scrutinized and fixed. But our government has proven time and again that they are not interested in the people of this country but only staying in power.

𝕱𝖊𝖉𝖊𝖗𝖆𝖑 𝕿𝖗𝖆𝖓𝖘𝖕𝖆𝖗𝖊𝖓𝖈𝖞

Also, there needs to be significantly more transparency. Classified briefings aside, each decision-making process should be recorded and archived for the American people to see. Before a decision is made the American people must be allowed to review the process. If our decision makers knew that every word was being scrutinized, they would choose them wisely. There should also be a video made to explain each initiative in layman's terms to ensure Americans know what is happening. Each discussion needs to include subject matter experts to ensure our leaders are making the correct decisions because being elected to an office, in no way, qualifies you to make decisions or magically makes you an expert. It really is amazing that we hold our elected officials in such high regard when the only thing they did was get more votes than the other candidate.

Government is also an inherent naysayer. People who work for the government are trained to say "no". No to new initiatives, no to spending more on valid programs, no to increased efficiency, no to cutting budgets of unnecessary programs, etc.

Education

As I state elsewhere in this book, the U.S. education system is broken, and no one is interested in fixing it. Mainly because it seems impossible but, we need to revamp the education system to instill a love of learning instead of a fear of testing. The idea of "grades" and traditional "progression" is antiquated. Children need to learn, not have anxiety about passing tests. They need to be excited about the subjects. There should definitely be evaluations to check the progress of the students, but it should be as they go, not a cumulative exam after everything has been taught. This is just one option, I'm sure there are others, but the main focus should be ensuring children are educated properly before moving to the next level. Unfortunately, as I stated, no one is interested in the individual student. They simply want to push kids through knowing that not every kid will be set up for success after they graduate.

The Department of Education needs to either be reorganized, downsized, or disbanded. Either that or they need to recruit its members from the "front lines" of education (teachers). There should be Federal Representatives from each state that are immersed in the educational process of their state to ensure the Federal level is properly informed. If you solicit help from anyone else, you run the risk of hiring a "spotlighter" or someone who is only interested in getting recognition instead of actually helping. It's sad how most administrators think they have to change something or spend money to be successful when all they really need to do is listen to their schools and help them achieve their goals. Instead, you get self-serving "woke" "intellectuals' who think they know better than everyone else. It really is sad to see so much time, money, and effort wasted on frivolous programs that don't actually benefit the students.

Another issue with the education system in this country is that the school "year" is not conducive to working parents. There are too many days off and the children should go to school through the summer. This would decrease summer learning loss and solve the childcare issue for families during the summer break.

Early outs are also a significant hindrance to working families, single parents, etc. They disrupt the tight, and fragile, schedule most families use to make everything work. How does the school district, state, federal government justify making families adjust their schedule periodically so the school can have a teacher's workshop, etc. What is a family supposed to do when their child usually gets out of school at 3:30 but, on occasion, they get out at 1:30 or 2:00? Now the parents must either get off work early, and possibly lose leave/sick days, or lose pay. This is what I mean when I say the Administrators don't have the best interests of the children in mind when they make their decisions.

𝔙𝔬𝔱𝔦𝔫𝔤

We seriously can't figure out how to streamline voting? Everyone has a social security number. One SSN, one vote, period. This ensures that only U.S. citizens vote. Why can't we vote online? Corporations have state-of-the-art computer systems that safeguard your information. The Federal Government should be able to create a computer system, or use existing technology, where everyone can vote online using their SSN. Or we could shift the election cycle to line up with tax season. When you file your tax return you also vote. If you don't file a return, you don't vote.

Pharmaceutical Issues

We need to figure out a way for people to obtain affordable prescription drugs while continuing to encourage drug innovation. I think both are equally important but there are those who feel that, if we don't allow drug companies to overcharge for their products then they will stop innovating thereby reducing the amount of effective prescription drugs. There are many ways to remedy this issue but the one that comes to mind is to rearrange the federal budget to free up money to assist these companies. Another solution is to ask the best pharmaceutical scientists to work for the government as private contractors or DOD civilians. The pay would still be commensurate with their abilities/work, but we could ensure the cost to the consumer remains low. This would also allow us to let other companies manufacture the same drugs to drive prices down. As it stands, the prescription drugs are patented which prevents anyone else from manufacturing them thereby driving up the cost. Another factor that prevents us from controlling how prescription drugs are made and distributed is that China controls much of our prescription drug trade, among many other things.

There are also plenty of generic drugs that are often overlooked to make more money for the pharmaceutical companies. Also, we are now finding that generic drugs are being made by unscrupulous companies that lie about how their drugs are made and thereby disseminating substandard drugs. If the U.S. took over generic drug manufacturing and distribution, we could ensure they were made correctly and sold cheaply. This could be paid for by the profits from the drugs, costing the taxpayer nothing. However, a lot of these drugs would become unnecessary if we focused more on physical fitness and eating correctly.

China

How have we allowed China to control so much of our country? Well, because it makes good business sense. Our government has made it so difficult and expensive to manufacture items here that most companies have resorted to overseas production. Look at any product and more often than not it was made in China. The little "Made in China" stickers are everywhere. How could this have happened? How does a superpower, a superpower that used to be number one, allow another superpower to undermine them as much as China has us and still allow China to be so vital to our economic survival? Fair trade and diplomacy are absolutely necessary, but we also need to ensure we're not being taken advantage of.

Immigration

I believe we should allow any immigrant who wants to work to obtain a work visa and come into this country. We need good, hard-working immigrants in the U.S., but we also need to ensure they contribute to the country by paying a portion of what they make to the government. This sounds like paying taxes but it's more like a fee to come here and work. They should not be allowed to vote until they become citizens, but they should be allowed to take advantage of some of the benefits of living in the U.S. If they want to work here, they should be fingerprinted, photographed, investigated, and provided with an identification card. They must also have a plan before they enter the U.S. This information should be kept in a database to ensure we know who exactly is in this country. If there are those who come here and do not obtain the proper credentials then they should be assessed to see if they are an asset to the U.S. and, if they are not, they should be deported to their home country. I doubt there will be many immigrants who fall into the latter category but, if they do, then they are probably here for unscrupulous reasons and need to leave anyway. A large problem is the lack of ICE and/or border patrol agents. We need to allot more funding to not only our border security and enforcement but border operations as well. I'm the last person to get upset about the way we treat those who enter the country illegally because those people chose to come here but, the way we run our border detention centers seems inefficient and must be overhauled/streamlined. This takes money and resources. People complain about the treatment of illegals, yet they don't want to spend money to properly handle the situation. The bottom line though is that we can't allow illegal immigration because bad people come across too. It's the job of the federal government to ensure the safety of its citizens and letting anyone in without documenting them first is failing at that job. We need to streamline the path to citizenship, simplify it, and increase the number of people working on approving citizenships. Increase the number of people working on immigration issues. U.S. citizens complain so much about illegal immigration, yet no one does anything substantial about it.

We also need to work better with Mexico to solve the immigration issue. It should be a joint effort to ensure the safety of both our country's citizens. There should be more official border crossing points with both countries occupying a station on their respective side of the border. We should solicit help from Mexico to discourage illegal border crossings and encourage legal ones. Mexico should prepare its citizens for crossing our border so when they get to our side, they need only be printed and photographed for our database before they can be sent on their way.

Issues to pursue

Issue 1: Space

At the time of this writing, the private sector has partnered with the U.S. Government to restart the space program. This is long overdue. Yes, there is an argument to keep humans on one planet, so we don't pollute another one but, I don't think that concern outweighs the need to explore. Pushing farther out into space allows us to explore more of it. Why wouldn't we want to invest in creating new technologies that may someday allow us to explore the outer reaches of our solar system, and beyond? Also, it would be amazing to make space travel available to all. It seems extraneous and unnecessary but life is about living and doing as many amazing things as you can, why wouldn't we try? Especially given the increased interest by the private sector. Having private corporations involved with space travel, like everything else, will increase efficiency and probably produce

a far superior product.

Issue 2: Farming

There is a growing problem in this country regarding the availability, and quality, of food. While industrial farming has provided many advantages, it doesn't seem to be enough. There are also concerns about overuse of chemicals, etc. Perhaps it's time to focus on not only industrial farming but sustainable farming as well. If we continue to abuse the land for the current generation, there might not be land available for future generations. I believe it's important to focus on both equally. Those who are here now must be cared for, but it can't be at the cost of our children, grandchildren, etc. We must insist that agriculture be productive and beneficial to the world while not destroying the land on which it uses to grow. Some think that if we continue to conduct industrialized farming that the land will become unusable in the very near future, thereby leaving us with no means to grow food.

Issue 3: Guns

Guns are a divisive subject in this country and I'm not sure why. The 2nd Amendment clearly states that *"the right of the people to keep and bear Arms, shall not be infringed"*. This doesn't mean that you can bear arms sometimes or only in certain places, this means it's your right to bear arms. There are those who post signs in certain places stating that bearing arms is prohibited. By whose authority? The constitution allows us to bear arms and I believe it takes more than a sign to change that. Having signs such as these begs the question: Why? Why are they prohibiting a person's right to bear arms in that location/situation? Are they fearful that someone will use it? Are they fearful that a crime may be committed by the person bearing arms? A sign will not stop a criminal from committing crime, if that were true all shop owners should put up "robbing prohibited" signs instead. The fact is that when you put up a sign attempting to violate a citizen's 2nd Amendment rights you put them in danger and make them vulnerable to those who would not abide by a sign. It's odd that this needs to be

explained.

Issue 4: Incentivizing Charity

There is a lot of charity work being done but it doesn't seem to be enough. We need to make it lucrative for people to be charitable. There may already be programs in place, but they clearly aren't doing enough. There needs to be an aggressive effort to ensure a corporation, before they can operate in an area, has done something to help the less fortunate in the community. Some examples: The Starbucks Community Center, The Tesla Sports Complex, The Amazon Homeless Shelter, or the Disney Foster Home. These corporations make billions, why not ask them to help those less fortunate?

Yes, I believe we should invest in foster homes. There are too few foster families for the number of foster children in this country. If we make a state-of-the-art foster home with all the amenities a child needs, we can make it a positive experience and help these kids who normally wouldn't have an advantage over those in a family setting. The facilities could have classes on finance, fitness, and other life lessons. They could have tutors on staff to assist with homework. Comfortable facilities that make a child feel welcome and comfortable and a staff that has been vetted and cleared to ensure those caring for foster children are doing it for the right reasons and not just to get a paycheck. These facilities need staff that truly care for the children and has their best interest at heart. Most importantly, the staff must have the ability to put the child's needs above their own, at least while they're at work.

ISSUES THAT NEED WORK

1. Hungry American Children – figure out a way to tap into the 150,000 tons of food wasted each day and disseminate it to, at least, hungry children.

2. Educational Inequality – subsidies for those less fortunate communities.

3. Vertical Farms – dig deeper to determine its worth.

4. Homelessness – get them off the street and into a bed.

5. China, Russia, Iran, North Korea – work to mitigate tensions, increase good will, and prevent conflict.

6. Child Protection Agencies – should be standardized across the U.S. to streamline procedures, interstate transfers, etc.

7. Military Spending – must be scrutinized. There is a lot of waste that still occurs, and it is not with the lower units. The massive waste is usually at the highest levels of the military yet lower levels are always forced to suffer first. This results in a lack of training, equipment and overall preparedness for combat. Also, a look at the

Defense Commissary Agency must be taken to ensure it is performing as necessary.

Global Competition

We don't consider other countries our "enemies" or "adversaries" anymore, we call them "competitors", it's less combative that way. The problem is our "competitors" still see us as adversaries and are actively working to weaken us, and possibly "destroy" us. Not destroy as in wanton destruction but destroy us from the inside out, politically, socially, and economically and, given the current political climate, they just might succeed.

For a long time, the U.S. was the big kid on the block. Even after Vietnam we were still very much a, if not the, superpower. As time went on, we focused more and more on fighting each other. It seems we've lost our edge, or at least our status as the big kid on the block. While we (the Government) were preoccupied with fighting with the other political party, other countries have figured out how to unify their leadership, and flourish. I see Japan growing stronger every day and think that they really have turned themselves around over the decades. Now they're the third-largest economy in the world with no signs of slowing. Pretty good for a country that was part of the Axis and bent on world domination. Maybe they still are but have changed their tactics? Either way, they are doing very well, and I can't remember ever hearing anything about government infighting, or political scandals, etc. It's as if they are focused on making Japan better instead of lining their own pockets?

Another country that seems to be doing well, and getting better by the year, is China. Granted, they manipulate their currency and utilize questionable, and sometimes "illegal" (according to whom?) business practices to ensure their growth but, the point is they are doing what is best for China, not the individual legislator. This allows them to grow at an alarming rate and they will probably overtake the U.S. and rise to the number one slot shortly.

Only recently have we been "fighting back" against countries and entities that are a detriment to our country. Prior to this effort we simply complained about how "unfair" it is while our competitors ignored our whining and grew stronger. Also, our "leaders" seem to think polarizing and dividing us is the best course of action when they should be unifying us. When your "leaders" focus more on alienating half of the country instead of attempting to bring both sides together, you have to question the motives of those "leaders". I sometimes wonder if it's simple incompetence, that our leaders simply don't know how to do their job well and are just fumbling through, faking like they know how to lead.

It's embarrassing how incompetent our legislative branch looks, I can't imagine how the world sees us, this sideshow bickering about petty issues, holding frivolous hearings, lining their pockets while their constituents are homeless in feces ridden streets.

Our country has taken itself for granted for far too long and it's time we started coming together on federal level initiatives at least to ensure we will continue to have a country to take for granted. Yes, there will always be issues on which Americans disagree, but preserving, and improving, the country should never be one of them.

When I become president, I'm going to treat every country as an equal, and as a friend. Now, sometimes friends get in disagreements and have arguments. I don't know a single friend I've ever had that I didn't have some sort of argument with at one time or another. Sometimes friends actually get in fistfights when the other friend steps out of line. If we stepped out of line sometimes you got tightened up a little bit. But that's not to say we couldn't be friends afterwards. I mean look at the 40s. Who would have thought that Germany and Japan would've been such close allies of ours after what happened back then?

People get too dramatic, and they see the world as it was 50 or 100 years ago or even two hundred years ago. It's not the same. We're all here to prosper, we're all here to get better, we all want our country to be the best, so we're cordial to each other. But we hold our own. It should be a secret that we're trying to be better than the next guy, it's a competition, after all, and that's what it should be all about. Healthy competition is good if they're trying to get better. We're all trying to get better. Their success pushes us which pushes them. Sometimes we may do something that's a tad untoward, but we shouldn't do anything too shady, and we can tolerate it if you're doing something that's technically legal but kind of a jerk move. If an ally of ours does something that crosses the line and hurts our people or hurts our country then yes, we're going to retaliate, or at least discuss it and figure out what the deal is and go from there. But no country is our "enemy" and anybody that says that doesn't understand people or how the world works. Now, people may consider us their enemy, and that's on them, that's their problem, but as far as we're concerned everybody gets a fair shake and tightened up as necessary.

Social Security vs. Social Programs

I don't claim to be an expert but, from everything I've read about Social Security, it's hanging on by a very thin thread. Due to more people retiring than paying in (and longer life spans) SS is not sustainable. As president, I will do whatever I can to stop broken systems like SS that have plagued this nation for decades. We have proven that we can generate funds out of "thin air" (seemingly) so I think we can come up with something to fix SS. Off the top of my head, we immediately stop deducting from everyone at the time of this effort and generate funds elsewhere to cover those who have already reached the "retirement" age. We should also refund the money to those who choose that option and keep the rest to accrue interest but not take any more from anyone.

Another option would be to overhaul it and find a better way to invest the money to ensure a better rate of return. This could be done by the government, but a better option would be to hire a successful investment firm and give

Americans the option to invest with the "government" (through a private, successful, firm) or keep the money to invest for themselves. A solely government-run program is rarely a good option, so we need more private, successful, businesses involved to ensure prosperity.

Now, on the other hand if you are receiving anything from the government there must be a system in place to repay that debt. Simply giving "free money" to anyone is bad business and will only result in more debt – or higher taxes. Neither of these are optimal unless the government is getting something for their money. The government doesn't owe anyone anything except safety, interstate infrastructure, and other things you might not be able to procure on your own. Everything else should be provided by state/local governments or procured yourself.

Now, there is something to be said about providing people with basic survival needs but it isn't sustainable without some kind of payback method. If you are unable to procure your own food, water, and/or shelter then there should be a program to help but in return you should have to provide some sort of service. Otherwise, other taxpayers, who are taking care of themselves, are expected to take care of you as well. It's not fair to those who are self-sustaining to pay for others who are not. This is where the "payback" services could help. Whatever talent the person receiving the government support has can be used to help others. This talent may be as simple as sweeping floors or picking up garbage, but it will help those whose taxes are being used to help.

Another option would be to record the debt and have the receiver pay it back when they get on their feet. However, this could take an exorbitant amount of time and almost defeats the purpose of providing these services without cost unless the receiver becomes very successful. Perhaps a small payment each month to assist in the cost of the services? Although, I don't know if that would be better than the citizen performing an actual service for their community. Either way, if you receive assistance from the government, it means you are receiving assistance from your fellow citizens, and it isn't fair to them that they must pay for themselves and you.

Privatization

Speaking of assistance from the government, I will also begin an initiative to make it lucrative for big businesses to take over government programs like welfare, social security, department of education, FDA, FAA, etc. These corporations will not have full control, as there will be government oversight from a small agency comprised of personnel with varying viewpoints who all have equal voting rights on how things should progress. This will ensure no partisan bias is influential in the decisions being made. The corporations will run their respective agencies as they would their own corporation to reduce waste and improve efficiency. We already use private corporations to run some of our government programs. TRICARE, for instance, is subcontracted to several different companies throughout the U.S. Each "region" operates separately from the others and changes subcontractors every couple of years. I think privatizing more government agencies, with a very small government oversight office, would lower costs, eliminate fraud, waste, and abuse, and ultimately provide a better "product" for the customer...us.

The plan is to provide tax incentives for those companies that take over the operation of a government program or division. For instance, Google will receive a tax break, or some other government incentive to take over the department of education. A small, diverse, federal agency will provide oversight, but Google would run day-to-day operation of the department. Government agencies are notoriously run poorly, and I believe that the right leadership, and vision, could produce excellent results. While government leaders have tried to appoint successful people, the infrastructure is to blame for the failings. Yes, a good leader should be able to motivate the people who work for them to succeed but the innerworkings of government agencies squash any hope of innovation or incentive to lean forward and go above and beyond.

Politics also plays a large role in the substandard practices of government agencies. Every four to eight years a different "leader" is appointed to these agencies based on their political affiliation which means that the whole system has to be overhauled to fit the new party's agenda. If private corporations ran federal programs, there would be no change in the innerworkings of the departments as they would have no political ties.

The Justice System

The best option for everyone (except judges and lawyers) is to avoid the justice system altogether. It has become a cesspool of corruption, indolence, and complacency and is only advantageous to those with money. Those of us who must use it are either left paying obscene amounts of money to a person who can't guarantee success or spending an exorbitant amount of time conducting research and drafting paperwork on our own.

It's absolute lunacy that a person can pay a lawyer tens, sometimes hundreds, of thousands of dollars and still lose. How is that right? The rules of the justice system are so convoluted that it's nearly impossible for a "layman" to successfully navigate it. As president I would work with lawmakers to standardize and simplify the justice system. I would make it so judges and lawyers don't profit from the ignorance and/or inability of a regular citizen just trying to receive justice. A person may have presented a valid, and legal, argument but if they didn't file the proper paperwork or failed to say a very specific thing, etc. then they lose the case. We talk about universal health care, free college, etc. why not the legal system? Heck, you can't even file a complaint without paying a filing fee, I mean, what is the purpose of the fee?! Aren't the people already being paid to process paperwork like this? Where does the money go? How is it being used? I'm told it's to buy computers or paper, etc. But shouldn't the state and/or federal government be paying for those items? Why does a citizen have to pay for a right granted to them by the constitution? Because "We The People" have allowed them to. We need to demand "Universal Legal Care", so normal people aren't continually raked over the coals by people who are trained to manipulate.

The legal system has become bastardized just like everything else. It is designed to make lawyers money by having frivolous hearings, pre-trial hearings, omnibus hearings, calendar calls, etc. The system seems set up to get the defendant and the plaintiff in the courtroom as much as possible as if to enable the lawyers to charge more fees? Why aren't all those things done in one day or via email? The legal system needs to be revamped and streamlined. There is too much bureaucracy and wasted time. When I worked for the state and had to go to court for a case, half the time the lawyers weren't ready, and we had to reschedule immediately. We're talking about parents who have lost their children and the lawyers were ill prepared to talk about the case and the rescheduled hearing would not be in a day or so but weeks later. To a judge or lawyer this may not mean anything, but to a parent a day is too much let alone weeks! I used to feel so bad for the parents. Some may have deserved to have their child taken from them, but they also deserved to be heard. Not all of them were guilty and to delay the reunion of a family because a lawyer is ill prepared is unforgiveable, yet it happened all the time. The saddest part is the incompetence was not only allowed but seemed to be fine to the judge. The fact is that they were all lawyers at one time and rig the system in their favor, not the people they are meant to serve.

One last thing about lawyers is how they allow for "loopholes" in the law to win cases. It's appalling how everything else could be right but one small aspect is incorrect or not according to a specific law or procedure and either the criminal walks or the person in the right loses the case. Common sense doesn't seem to be entertained in a courtroom as long as the proper procedures are followed. Doesn't seem right.

INITIATIVES

This section is dedicated to things I'd like to see implemented during my presidency. They may seem farfetched but so did the abolition of slavery and women's rights at one time. The only limitations we have are those we allow.

Citizens born with lethal conditions

For instance, there are many people born with afflictions that the majority of us never have to endure. There are also children who develop afflictions that are out of anyone's control. I believe these afflictions should be taken care of by a government fund specifically for that purpose. This could be funded by donations, an alternate funding stream, or possibly even taxes but a child shouldn't have to suffer due to something no one could control. Obviously, we would have to determine the severity of these afflictions to determine who "needs" care. I believe all children need help, but I don't think it's fair that a non-lethal, non-debilitating, or "non-costly" affliction should be taken care of by the government. I put "non-costly" in parenthesis because that can be relative to the family's financial situation so those cases will be taken case-by-case. There are non-lethal afflictions that can be costly to a family, and I don't think there is anything wrong with helping those people. This will need to be well defined to avoid abuse. Stipulations must be

put in place to ensure corruption doesn't occur in the future.

Feminine "Issues"

In the same vein as "things people can't control", I think it's unfair that a woman should have to pay for her feminine hygiene products. This may seem out of left field but, after having lived in a house full of women, I have developed a deep sense of empathy for what women go through each month. It's downright unfair they have to endure such tribulations regularly and any help we can give them might ease that burden, at least a little. Offering free feminine hygiene products is a very logical step to help those who had no choice in which gender they would be and the inherent trials that accompany it.

𝕳olidays

Another change I would make would be for all federal holidays to be observed on Fridays (or Thursdays if I am able to implement a 4-day work week). Additionally, I would make the following Monday a work holiday to give everyone a four- or five-day weekend, depending on the work schedule we have at the time.

Alternate Work Locations

Due to the lessons we've learned from COVID-19 regarding the ability for most Americans to telework, I would implement alternate work locations. This means if you don't absolutely have to be at work to do your job, you can work from anywhere, provided you have adequate telephone and email service.

If COVID-19 is still a threat, for those personnel who must come into work, we will reconfigure workspaces to accommodate social distancing and/or create isolated work areas. We could do this by building up cubicles or putting acrylic glass around each workstation. Obviously, this wouldn't work for all federal positions, but we will implement this course of action wherever feasible.

Teleworking would also alleviate a person's need to highlight that they came in early, stayed late, worked the weekend, etc. I find it odd that people brag about these things. Are they trying to impress? It always seems to have the opposite effect, especially if the person's co-workers are doing comparable work. Are the people who work long hours and weekends wasting time during normal work hours or are they trying to get ahead? If it's the latter, then that hard work will get noticed naturally without them highlighting their efforts. The results will show that they put in the extra work for the betterment of the company/mission/etc. but some are so insecure, or guilty, that they feel the need to tell everyone about their "extra effort". This usually results in co-workers resenting the person for being a "spotlighter" and the boss thinking they are just being obsequious. It's always better to be a "silent professional" for their reward is exponentially greater than the "spotlighter". It shows that you have a higher purpose than just getting noticed and will speak volumes about your character. But the trick is not to do it for this reason either. Adopting a selfless attitude and the satisfaction of accomplishing your goals will be rewarding enough, everything else is extra.

Now, if you are specifically asked through direct feedback, a performance report, etc., then you must fight the urge to be humble for this is an acceptable time to highlight your hard work. Supervisors expect you to forgo your humility and talk openly about your efforts so they can properly assess, and possibly reward, you for the good you've done for the unit/team/business.

The time for recognition will come naturally, don't force it or you will look like that is your only reason for doing the work. If that is the case then you may want to find a different line of work, one that will allow you to be fulfilled by the effort, not the appreciation.

Voting

Why is it so hard to believe that the U.S. voting is flawed? Our elections have been controlled by people with money for centuries. Also, it is run by people, meaning not entirely automated, and extremely "loose" (a term we used in the military to describe a person or persons who weren't squared away). There is so much potential (and confirmed proof) that the system is affected by social media, human error, human meddling, etc. that it is laughable to think it's infallible. Also, the U.S. has been meddling in other countries' elections for decades, how could we possibly think ours is immune? China and Russia need only hire a company to flood social media with propaganda supporting the side they think will be most malleable to them.

The way we vote in this country must be revamped and streamlined. There is too much room for error and those errors matter in tight races. How are we still using pen and ink to cast votes, relying on humans to count those votes, not associating each vote with a social security number, and allowing "mail-in" ballots? I'm not talking about absentee ballots that people request and are then sent, I'm talking about hundreds of thousands of unsolicited ballots mailed out (sometimes in duplicate and triplicate) to people that may or may not be receiving them. How do we guarantee that the person sending in the ballot is the person on the ballot? The truth is there is no way to be sure and this is by design, this allows for manipulation of the results. It's lunacy that we use the voting methods in place today. It's also crazy that each state has its own process. I am a firm believer in State's rights but when it comes to a federal issue that affects the entire country, the process should be standardized. The federal government must create a web site where a person logs in, enters their social security number, and votes. It can be a secure server to which only a few trusted agents have access. A person would be able to log in at any time and check the status of their vote to ensure it was cast for the candidates they chose. The voting could be open for a week before election day to allow for the servers to handle the traffic. Then, on election day, at 11:59 pm Hawaii Standard Time, you'll have a definitive answer regarding the election. If the states wanted to maintain control, they would be provided a similar system strictly for their state, but it would be overseen and checked by a federal agency.

I believe the voting system we currently have is by design and meant to allow for manipulation and ambiguity to allow for "tweaking" as deemed necessary by whoever has the means. I know, this sounds far-fetched and "tin foil hat"-ish but, as I said, the U.S. has been controlling elections in other countries for years, why is it so hard to believe that we would control our own?

𝔚𝔬𝔯𝔩𝔡𝔴𝔦𝔡𝔢 𝔍𝔫𝔳𝔢𝔰𝔱𝔦𝔫𝔤

We occupy a lot of space in this world but how much of it do we actually own? How much of it can we use to generate income? Very little, if any. That doesn't seem like something "we" do. I'd like to change that. I would like to invest in real estate around the globe and actually own it and develop it to not only generate income for the U.S. but help those less fortunate to prosper. Just think if we could build up an impoverished part of the world and make it profitable? Or buy real estate here in the U.S. and run it like a business. I'm sure there's a law or rule against this but why? Why rely on the people to fully fund the government?

Another option would be to invest in a hedge fund, or hire a hedge fund manager to invest our money, etc. Again, I'm sure there are "rules" or "laws" against it but those can be changed. Why not put our money to work for us instead of it being wasted by the government? How much better for the government to be self-sustaining and not need tax money to operate? People forget that the income tax hasn't always been around. Although it started during the Civil War, it wasn't official until 1913 when our "leaders" all voted for the 16th amendment. They tried it before in 1894 but the Supreme Court struck it down as unconstitutional, however just like all horrible ideas, the legislative branch kept it alive, acted autonomously, and ratified the 16th amendment.

It's typical, lazy, progressive thinking that we can tax our way out of debt, relying on others to help instead of helping ourselves. The government expects Americans to do this, yet they won't. It's too hard to draft legislation or too far above them to figure out the details. They would rather stay with the same status quo and not balance the budget, go further in debt, and betray their constituents. If there are laws against it, change the laws. If there is an amendment preventing this action, repeal it. Unfortunately, our current "leaders" lack the proper courage and drive to do what's necessary for the good of the country.

𝔓𝔯𝔦𝔳𝔞𝔠𝔶

Due to invasive tech companies, public and private cameras (security, traffic, etc.), and everyone having the ability to record you at any moment, it seems like a person's privacy is rapidly eroding. If a person is in a public place, they should instinctively know that they can be observed, recorded, and scrutinized at all times. However, if a person is in a "private" place, whatever that may be, their privacy should be aggressively guaranteed. While I think this is mostly prevalent in our society, I think it should include electronic devices and, if that privacy is violated, the punishment must be so severe that it isn't worth the trouble of doing it in the first place.

A person should be afforded the right to privacy whenever they want when in their private residence. The only exception to this rule would be if the person is suspected of a crime but, even then, the stipulations must be very clear and relatively stringent so as not to erroneously target the wrong person. The point is unless you're in your own home, expect to be watched by the world, and act accordingly. If you are home alone then your privacy should be as protected as your life. No one other than law enforcement should be able to monitor a person in their home. People are exposed enough and should have a safe haven from any and all prying eyes and ears.

𝕸𝖔𝖓𝖊𝖞

Why does the federal government continue to issue pennies and nickels? They lose about $69-85m dollars a year making pennies and the nickel (5¢) costs 7¢ each which costs us another $33m. So, why do we still do it? Yes, we make up the deficit with dimes and nickels but, wouldn't it be more responsible to cease production of the penny and nickel and put the extra $100m to some good use? I've heard it's to keep prices low, but is it? Wouldn't it be easier to just round up anyway? A lot of stores have been asking if we want to round up to help the local food bank, or COVID relief, etc., why not implement that as a way for the government to make some extra money? Get rid of the penny and nickel and mandate that all purchases will be rounded up to the nearest dollar and that extra change will be given to the government? I'm sure that would add up to a pretty good chunk of change. Then we could do away with the income tax altogether. I think people would gladly accept paying a little more for each item for the ease of balancing their budget and not having their paycheck taxed.

Speaking of money, I would ensure that the military's financial process is streamlined. The bureaucratic red tape that exists in the military's contracting world is abhorrent, often to the point whereby the time an item is sourced, built, and shipped, it is obsolete or no longer needed. Pieces of equipment arrive at units after something far better has been created. Buildings are erected so slowly that thousands of training hours are wasted waiting for them to be completed. Heck, there have been whole military bases constructed that have immediately been abandoned due to shifting priorities.

This isn't always the case though. In special operations, for the most part, funds are allocated, kit is purchased, and buildings are erected in a timely manner because they use common sense and aren't fully controlled by the "bean counters". Usually, these initiatives have the backing of a high-ranking officer who can expedite the effort but that begs the question, why can't all the projects be expedited if it just takes a few high-ranking officers to authorize it? Things can happen quickly in the military, if it's important enough to the person making the decisions. What they don't realize is that other units are trying to do their mission but don't have the luxury of a general helping them, so they plod along, doing their mission with substandard equipment.

Yes, the "bean counters" will call me naïve and say that "there is only so much money to go around" and "we must prioritize what we get" but to that I say ask for more. Make the effort to highlight the needs of those you serve. "Bean counters" either don't know, or don't care what happens on the "front lines" and it shows.

When I say "bean counters" I'm not talking about the unit level comptrollers, I'm talking about higher level personnel who fancy themselves more important than the warfighter because they hold the "purse strings". I've seen these people in budget meetings scoff and deny initiatives because they don't fully understand the gravity if the initiatives aren't funded. I've seen warfighters denied training and equipment in order to fund the politically attractive effort, efforts that usually cost way too much money for what their worth and will, potentially, prepare the command for the future, although the chances of it actually coming to fruition, let alone helping is 50/50. It's usually some "leader's" vision of the future that they won't be around to see implemented because they will have moved on to another job before the initiative is completed, if at all. What can happen is the "champion" of the effort is assigned somewhere else and the initiative is left to atrophy because no one who cares is there to see it through.

Initiatives

𝔐𝔦𝔩𝔦𝔱𝔞𝔯𝔶

There are certain things that I would change regarding how the president uses the military. I don't mean defending the nation, armed conflict, etc., I'm talking about how each presidential candidate uses the military for political purposes. Promises to draw down troops in country "x", commitment of troops to effort "y", etc. I'm sure someone has an explanation about why we telegraph troop movements, draw downs, etc. but I don't think it's valid. No one has the right to know what we're doing with our troops besides the troops and their chain of command. While the American people think it is our right to know everything that goes on with the military, they are sorely mistaken. They only need to know that, hopefully, the government is using the military in a manner that is beneficial to the U.S., whatever that may be. Telegraphing troop movements or advertising strategies only allows the enemy to know what we're doing. Perhaps it's a ploy or misdirection to take the focus off some other operation but I firmly believe that we give away too much. How much do we know about China and their military exploits? What about Russia? The average person only knows what is found out because those two entities divulge next to nothing.

Do our leaders have a false sense of security, or a true one? It's hard to say, but when I see press conferences where reporters ask the press secretary if it's true that the president is going to draw down troops to a certain number in a certain area, it seems like we're putting the lives of those deployed in danger.

If I were in charge, most things we do regarding combat deployments would at least be "Controlled Classified Information" and possibly "Confidential" or "Secret". The less our "competitors" know about us the better. This not only allows us plausible deniability but a certain degree of mystery to keep our "competitors" on their heels.

𝕴𝕽𝕾

Do we really need the IRS? Do we need an organization that refuses to handle in person problems until they feel it's necessary and then do so with invasive audits? They have the manpower and time to send everyone who received a stimulus payment a letter in the mail (envelope, paper, stamp, etc.) but they can't answer questions?

We wouldn't need the IRS if we implemented the initiatives I mention elsewhere in this book. Taxes should be straightforward with no loopholes or breaks. Just flat taxes that are easy to pay and easy to track. A certain percentage should be taken out of each paycheck to alleviate the need for anyone to have to "do their taxes" each year. I would also eliminate things like capital gains taxes, etc. We need to find a way for the government to earn money, not just "make" it from its citizens.

A good way to "earn" money is to increase taxes on "nice to have" items. Citizens would get behind a law that let them keep more of their money and only be taxed if they chose to buy certain items. I'm sure there would be come controversy on what is deemed "necessary" but I'm sure we could boil it down and figure it out. Some people in our current government are both lazy and shady so they just go with what's easiest and what will most benefit them, not necessarily what's best for the American people. I get it, we need taxes for interstate issues, etc. but it just seems like the easy way out. Let elected officials earn that hefty paycheck and actually do something for us, not just keep the status quo, AKA: the path of least resistance.

For those who say, "you just don't understand" or "well, that's not how it works", are no better than those who can't figure out workable solutions that serve the people. Yes, that's the way the "system" works now because those "in power" have made it that way. There is nothing stopping them from changing the system, they are literally the only ones who can change the system. Unfortunately, changing the current system won't benefit them and their donors so it doesn't get done. The only way to fix this problem is to vote everyone out and not vote for either political party. Yes, there will be growing pains but maybe that's what this country needs, a shake up, some free thinkers who aren't bogged down by "the way it's always been" and are free to make changes that make sense for everyone, not just those "in power". Alas, this country is terrible at coming together and only really does so when there's a major tragedy, which is also a tragedy. If only we could figure out how to put our stupid differences (perpetuated by the political parties) aside and come together for the issues that actually affect all of us.

Modification of the Electoral College

One of the biggest issues people have with the electoral college is that big cities don't normally vote the way the rest of the state does. If it weren't for those big cities, the state would usually vote for someone else. So, why don't the cities separate like Washington D.C., become their own entity, and have their own electoral votes? They could operate as D.C. does, thereby allowing the rest of the state to not be influenced (negatively or positively) by the tremendous populations of their biggest cities. It seems like a fair trade-off, and it would ultimately serve both sides or, at least make it fair in that most left leaning people seem to congregate to the major cities whereas center-right leaning people seem to spread out and want more individual space. Although, all this could be moot if we could find a candidate that didn't alienate half the country. Unfortunately, as long as we have two major parties, who wield far too much power and influence, we are stuck with this system.

The Future of the U.S.

The way things are going in the U.S. today it almost seems like someone (read: many somones) is intentionally distracting the citizens of the U.S. in order to weaken us. Our borders are porous, we aren't very focused on national security, we have a very odd foreign policy, and are constantly distracted with non-issues.

The U.S. seems to have lost focus on staying a superpower and is, instead, focused on ensuring no one ever experiences any adversity or hardship at the expensive of the future of the Nation. Meanwhile, China and Russia are expanding their empires, kind of overtly, while we continue to give up on that which we've spent blood and treasure. For instance, at the time of this writing, the U.S. has pulled completely out of Afghanistan almost intentionally to make room for China to move in to continue its mining, among other, operations. They have also gradually made a significant presence in Africa, an untapped resource, another resource that we can't figure out. We're adequate at occupying other regions and looking for terrorists but we are terrible at nation building and getting a return on our investment. Well, I say "we" but really I mean the government, which has become a mechanism for businesses to become stronger while the country grows weaker. Not that I'm against business, on the contrary, I believe business is the answer but only if used properly. Our government continues to help businesses yet doesn't do anything for the people of the country. But I digress, unless we (the government) start getting in the game, and expanding OUR empire, we're going to cease being a superpower and more of a pawn (not that we haven't become that already).

The scary thing about what I mentioned above is that half of the country is on board with what is happening. They've wanted the U.S. to be knocked down a few pegs due to the history of the nation. According to them, the U.S. deserves the strife it's experiencing. Too many white men, not enough of, literally, anything else. Well, why does the

U.S. have to grow weaker for those "oppressed" to grow stronger? I'm all about equality and diversity but not at the cost of our country's basic values – life, liberty, and the pursuit of happiness. This country has always been about freedom and prosperity, but neither one of these comes easily or without some cost. Unfortunately, we have become this beacon of light for everyone yet failed to remind everyone how we got here. Instead, we have leaders bowing to the demands of an entitled populace who demand everything be given to them for free while they do nothing to earn it. This briefs really well but, beyond that, it doesn't make sense. The country was forged on the blood, sweat, and tears of those willing to work for it. In order for this country to stay great it must be inhabited by people who share this same work ethic. Unfortunately, those looking for a free ride are increasing, and it is mainly due to some people in our government sharing these views. It doesn't matter to them that there are those of us who must pay more and work harder to support those who want these free things, they just want votes and votes come from people, people who receive things from those candidates.

The bottom line, it's futile to reason with those who seem like they're against the country because that's exactly what they are. They think the policies that are a detriment to the thriving of this country are a good thing and that "we" (our country) has never been good or right, aside from the incidences that fit their agenda. I don't understand why anyone would want to hurt the very place that has made them who they are. Some citizens of the U.S. will admit how they gained their prosperity, they simply want to condemn the very system that provided it.

Fortunately, right now we are, for the most part, doing pretty well. Maintaining the status quo as much as possible. Bettering our own lives as much as possible. All the while the U.S. is taken down, piece by piece, by some in the government. It doesn't affect us too much, right now, but what about the future? What about future generations? I guarantee that China will be here long after we're (the U.S.)

is gone if we don't do something now. I get a kick out of the people who fight for the climate but not the actual country. China couldn't care less about the environment and are untouchable. China does what it wants, when it wants, and has help from Russia and Iran. Meanwhile we bow down to every single thing that may make our politicians look bad. You can only be the benevolent giant for so long before the other giants, who couldn't care less about benevolence, grow stronger and take you out.

Most individuals who seek the presidency do so with aspirations of becoming powerful, getting rich, or being remembered in history, whereas I simply want to serve. I have no hidden agenda, personal ambitions, or secret motives behind my goal to become President, only to serve.

I believe this is what our country needs, citizens who genuinely want to serve and make a difference. Instead, we get spotlighters and self-servers who want to use the office for their own personal gain. We all know it, we all talk about it, yet we do nothing about it. We are perpetually left with only those who seek fame. It's obvious to everyone except those in "power". They can't wait to get on television so they can bad mouth the opposition in order to generate favor and, more importantly, votes for them and their side. It's almost as if we need those positions to be involuntary, so we can choose someone who should be in there, not just who "they" (the political parties) decide who should run.

This is why I think I would be a good president. I strive to solve problems and I don't care who gets the recognition. I believe a President should be a facilitator and give credit where it's due. I would actively find bi-partisan subject matter experts to solve any given problem or issue the American people are concerned with, highlight when that person solves the problem, and then aggressively implement the solution.

I care about people. I've been serving my whole life. I spent almost 24 years in the military, retired and then worked for the state of Alaska in child protection, then I became a contractor for the military, serving so our military members are prepared for war. I've been a Girl Scout leader, a swim coach and swim official, and a soccer coach. Honestly, I don't remember all the times I've volunteered because that's not why I do it. I volunteer because it's the right thing to do. If we all just pitched in a little bit, we'd all be a lot better off. For instance, I was talking to my sister-in-law the other day about my niece and nephew's PTA, and she stated they were raising five-digit amounts in just one of her fund raisers, and almost 6 digit amounts overall and it was because people came out and volunteered for that little local area. It's no surprise how some areas thrive, and others fail. It has everything to do with the people who live there and what they are willing to do to help. It takes a little bit of legwork, a little bit of elbow grease from everybody and things can be great. Just a little selflessness, a little not even a lot, can make all the difference.

So, I'm asking people to step up give a little bit back, not for recognition, not to get something out of it, not to show people how unselfish you are, but just because it's the right thing to do.

I don't drink alcohol, don't smoke, and I don't use drugs. I don't have any real hobbies other than spending time with my family so I don't have a lot of distractions that would keep me from my work. Most importantly, though, I genuinely care about helping others and ensuring that everyone gets a fair shake. The issues of this country have become overly complicated by design. Those "in charge" create impossible situations so they don't have to find real solutions. They are then left to campaign for reelection which was their goal all along. I hope that my actions will result in my reelection in order for me to continue my work to help America.

Made In America

Too often I hear people complain about goods not being manufactured in America. I also hear complaints about the horrible working conditions in the countries that corporations choose to use because of their cheap labor. I hear these things, but I don't hear a solution.

The solution, in my opinion, is to charge a fee to import goods from countries who condone "sweat shops". Make it cost prohibitive to bring things into this country if they come from a foreign factory that has harsh working conditions. To this you may say "but the companies will just pass on the costs to the consumer", and to that I say, probably, although I did hear Biden's press secretary say this wouldn't happen. She's wrong. The corporations will most certainly jack up their prices to compensate for the import taxes/fees.

To this I say, so what? Let them raise their prices. A couple of things may happen. Either people will still buy the products at elevated prices, which is not unheard of based on the price of cigarettes, or they will stop buying the products and the companies selling the products will either adapt or go out of business. Either way the government will receive supplemental income from the corporations which will help lower taxes on its citizens.

Now, I'm not talking about necessities. I'm simply talking about "luxury" items that people don't "really" need. People don't need an iPhone. They would love to have one and are already paying an exorbitant amount for one, but they absolutely don't need it. People also don't need Nike sneakers; they can grab some New Balances or Adidas.

The bottom line is that, unless the product is necessary for basic human survival, import taxes will be levied and companies will be forced to find a cheap way to manufacture their product in the states. This means more jobs for Americans, lower taxes for Americans, and invigorated American communities. I also think we'll find that Americans will pay the extra money for the product which is great for the economy.

Prison Reform

There is a real problem with prisons in this country. They don't seem very safe, they don't seem to rehabilitate very well (which should be the goal), and they cost an exorbitant amount of money (around $38 billion.)

There are probably plenty of reasons for these issues, the main being the same reason for our decaying educational system, underfunded/undertrained police force, etc., people simply don't care about these things. People usually only care about things that can do something for them or that affect them. Well, in the case of prison reform, I believe it will benefit everyone.

Border Enforcement

This may seem like an oversimplification, but it seems very simple. If someone crosses any of our borders illegally, then they have broken the laws of our country and should be punished accordingly. They shouldn't be released, they shouldn't be sent home, they should be held accountable for their actions.

Accountability would be manual labor. They would earn a wage like any U.S. prisoner, but they would do so in a prison type environment. There should be a set sentence for each offense and the sentences should increase with the number of attempts they make. If you want to stop illegal crossings, you have to make it undesirable to do so. Simply releasing them is only providing them a chance to do it again or take advantage of what the U.S. has to offer without truly earning it.

Yes, those who were born here didn't "earn" their citizenship, but they also have to adhere to the laws of this country. If a person begins their time in the U.S. with a felony it doesn't set a good stage for the future. Also, those coming here illegally are enjoying the freedom and opportunity but aren't' contributing to its upkeep. They are, essentially, getting a free pass.

All countries have borders, and those borders must be enforced to ensure that the people coming in aren't there to do harm and to ensure that they are positively contributing to society. Many other countries have learned the hard way about simply opening their borders and letting anyone in who is unchecked and/or undocumented. The result is unrest and violence.

As I've said before, I think everyone who wants to come here should, but they should do it the correct way. We need to dedicate more forces to the border and patrol it like we would any perimeter we don't want intruders to access. I'm talking about the full force of the federal government along the border. It's the only way to truly secure our country. We should minimize crossing points by building a virtually impenetrable barrier and patrol the barrier both on the ground and in the air. We spend so much time and money patrolling the skies in/around other countries yet don't fully dedicate what's necessary to our own. If you want real change you have to be willing to fully commit.

But that's if they really wanted change. I can't believe that anyone in our government is truly interested in closing the border, otherwise they would have done it already. No, I believe they pay a lot of lip service (both sides) to appease us and then do the bare minimum, if that. You need only speak to a border patrol agent to know how futile the effort is right now due to low manning and even lower resources.

Also, in addition to closing the border, we need to actually speak to the leaders of the countries from which these immigrants originate. I don't mean people who have no power, like the vice president, I mean really dig in and get to the root cause of the problem. Not saying we can solve all of the world's problems, but we should focus on those that directly affect us. In order to do this, we need to collect information about from where everyone originates, in addition to getting pictures of them, taking their fingerprints, and creating a file on them. Once we have that data, we can compile it and see from where the majority of them are coming and act accordingly. Imposing sanctions on those countries or actually investing in those countries, may be the answer. We either stop them from thriving or help them thrive even more so their people will be less apt to flee. Energizing the economy of a poverty-stricken country could be the catalyst needed for their citizens to prosper.

Border Enforcement Plan:

U.S./Mexico border policy:

- Phase 1: Deploy enough National Guard troops, DOT, DOJ, IRS, DOE, DOA, DHS, DOC, DOD, ICE, CBP, USSS, DOI personnel to the border to adequately augment the Border Patrol until a sufficient amount of Border Patrol agents can be procured.
    - U.S. Personnel will be split between actual border security (stopping illegal entry into the U.S.) and processing those who are attempting to enter the U.S. legally.
    - U.S. Personnel charged with processing those who wish to enter the U.S. legally will ensure that every legal entry candidate is:
        - Searched for weapons, drugs, or any other illegal contraband.
        - Photographed
        - Fingerprinted

- Issued an identification card to confirm that the individual has entered the country legally and is allowed to work, live, and pay taxes.

  - The card will be of the same quality as a "Real I.D." and/or military Common Access Card to prevent illegal fabrication.

  - The same database used for U.S. CACs will be used for legal immigrant I.D. cards.

  - If a legal immigrant loses their I.D. card a new one will be issued to them.

- Any U.S. employer who hires people who do not possess a valid form of I.D., will be severely punished.

- The number of border crossing points will be temporarily increased to accommodate the thousands of immigrants who cross the border each day.
- The legal immigrant will then:
  - Be equipped with a backpack with food, water, and other items that may be determined beneficial to them upon their entry into the U.S.
  - Be escorted to a holding area to await travel to their final U.S. entry site.
  - This final entry site will be determined based on factors such as:
    - Willingness of the location to accept them (i.e., Sanctuary states/cities), desire of the legal immigrant to go to that location, etc.
  - Board a vehicle that will either take them directly to their final entry site or a train station/airfield/etc. where they will board

another vehicle that will take them to their final entry site.

Phase 2: Deploy U.S. Navy Seabees, U.S. Army Corps of Engineers, and U.S. Air Force REDHORSE personnel to the border to construct a barrier between the U.S. and Mexico that will make it virtually impossible to cross into the U.S. illegally.

- o This barrier will have designated entry points built into it where the abovementioned U.S. Personnel will conduct their processing of legal immigrants.
- o The barrier must be impregnable enough to deter any attempts to circumvent the processing stations.

Phase 3: Negotiations will be held with Mexico to allow U.S. troops to deploy to Mexican border towns to assist in the security of the Mexico side of the border.

- o Troops will occupy border towns such as Juarez, Mexicali, Nogales, Tijuana, etc. where they will deter illegal immigration into the U.S. while simultaneously stimulating the economy of, and assisting with the improvement of, those locales.

- Civil, Public, and Government Affairs will identify shortfalls of the areas and assist with remedies.
- Air and Ground patrols will be conducted on the south side of the border between all U.S. border crossings to deter any illegal immigration activity, as well as locate any unauthorized crossing points.

Phase 4: All people attempting to enter the U.S. illegally will be detained and placed in a holding area on the north side of the border.

- o This holding area will have food, water, and medical personnel to address any issues.
- o These people will be placed on Mexican contracted busses and, with U.S. and Mexican ground and air escort, will be taken back into Mexico and turned in to the nearest law enforcement agency.

- All Phases will be executed as nearly simultaneously as possible.

- Every effort must be made to deter illegal entry into the U.S., but the main deterrence should be the overwhelmingly easy and humane method of legal entry.

- All people attempting to enter the U.S. legally will be treated with the utmost respect and kindness.

- All people attempting to enter the U.S. illegally will be met with non-lethal force to include, but is not limited to, Directed Energy and Electroshock Weapons.

  o If U.S. personnel are met with lethal force, they will be authorized to use lethal force to defend themselves.

- Funding for this effort will be addressed in a different section, but it will be a result of decreasing/eliminating extraneous programs and agencies and/or rerouting funds and personnel of other government agencies.

Good Stewards

One saying that is always used by our leaders but seldom, if ever, followed is "we have to be good stewards of the people's money". But "we", meaning the government, rarely does this. They talk a big game by denying lower-level personnel little perks like new office equipment or upsizing a rental car when on temporary duty, but when it comes to big ticket items, especially ones that they deem "mission essential", the sky is the limit. Those at the higher levels spend money frivolously on programs that may or may not come to fruition while refusing truly "mission essential" items to each level below them until the person on the "front line" is denied even the slightest advantage.

One of my goals as President will be to ensure that the thoughtless spending ceases, and we hold accountable the companies with whom the government does business. The government awards contracts to companies to build pieces of military gear that often aren't what we wanted or have taken so long to be developed that the technology is obsolete.

This is one of the reasons I loved special operations so much, they made every effort to stay ahead of the tech to ensure their warriors had the most advanced and, more importantly, useful pieces of kit available. The bureaucracy on the "conventional" side of the military is cumbersome and inefficient and often results in warriors having to settle for substandard equipment.

Our military's only saving grace is its people. They make do with what they receive and get the mission done, at times in spite of those above them who, by the way, often award the contracts for substandard gear based on future employment opportunities once they leave government service. It really is amazing the double standard, well, not that there is one, but that it is so blatantly obvious.

This frivolous spending isn't limited to airplanes and tanks, you would be appalled at the amount of money that is wasted on things like office equipment. They'll spend tens of thousands of dollars on a copying machine only to have it break shortly after it is delivered. Then they must pay for a "certified" repairman to come and fix it, at an additional cost. They also purchase different types of equipment, like copying machines, which take different toner forcing them to make several different purchases instead of buying identical items to streamline the process. But then the shipment will be delivered to the wrong address and the person receiving the items will either accept them and use them or leave them in a storage area until someone claims them which, could be a long time if the person who ordered the items has left the organization because the items took so long to be delivered and now no one is even aware of the missing shipment. You can probably guess that this last part is anecdotal, but it happens more than you think.

Another anecdotal occurrence is the fact that the government will spend millions of dollars to book hotels and rental cars for entire units instead of using that money to build a dormitory or hotel on the base. The money could be spent once and house hundreds of people and save millions of dollars, but because it's a "different pot of money", they can't. Temporary Duty money is different than Military Construction money and one can't be used for the other, even if it would save the government tens of millions of dollars.

Regarding equipment procurement, my goal will be to ensure that the government receives exactly what it has requested and only pays for fully approved products. The days of simply accepting a piece of equipment because the money has already been allocated will be over. This will apply at all levels. The government has its own research and development entities, perhaps it needs its own manufacturing section as well? I will also demand that the companies that provide the equipment provide all the proprietary property, software, and equipment. The days of selling a piece of kit to the government only to charge them a fee for every upgrade would be over. The government gets screwed on a regular basis by companies who unscrupulously sell the government an item knowing fully well it isn't what they ordered, only to charge them again for "upgrading" (read: making it functional) the item.

This leads me to my next plan to ensure the government is being a good steward of the people's money, nuclear power. At the time of this writing, I believe that the government is looking into procuring small nuclear reactors for some or all of its bases. This is an effort I would champion. Our government is already wasting millions, if not billions, of dollars a year on energy, microreactors could be the solution to that issue. The reactors will have to be built with the utmost care and scrutiny to ensure maximum safety. They will also need fail safes to prevent catastrophe, both intentional and unintentional. Done correctly, nuclear microreactors could save the government a substantial amount of money which could be used for other programs that actually help the American people.

The government must set the example for the people. This is why every federal building will be powered by nuclear energy and all state and local government will be encouraged, and subsidized, to do the same. For too long the federal government has had the "do as I say, not as I do" mentality which only enrages the people. This is apparent when they implement policies that hurt the majority of the people in this country, and they do it without any remorse. It really is amazing how simply being elected by a majority somehow transforms you into an all knowing being who must "take care" of those who voted for you.

It would be great if our elected leaders truly did what was right and just for all Americans. We complain about inflation, taxes, and joblessness yet we do little to nothing about it. Meanwhile those causing these issues maintain their comfortable standard of living, not affected by any of these failed policies, wasting our valuable time. I say wasting our time because we have to live through the tough times and hope it gets better. It's not fair that "We the People" should have to suffer while those causing the issues feel no negative effects. I guess that's what life is all about? Getting to a position where you are above the law and aren't affected by "normal" problems? It really seems that way because no one is actually doing anything substantial to solve problems. For instance, at the time of this writing, the cost of gasoline is extremely high and the only solutions I've heard are tapping into the country's oil reserves or doing nothing and blaming Russia for invading Ukraine. Forget about the fact that this issue started before the invasion and that we only get about 8% of our oil from Russia.

This is the issue; our government simply puts Band-Aids on gunshot wounds. They could do drastic things that would benefit the people like stop the gas tax, stop exporting the very resource we need (oil) so we have more of it, and hold the oil companies accountable. We all know the price of oil is based on speculation and no real facts, why can't our "leaders" do something about that? Because they'd rather implement quick fixes that look and sound good politically but don't have any real lasting effect.

Because who cares anyway? The news cycle will continue, and we'll be distracted by something else soon enough. Even if we aren't distracted by something else, what can we do about it? Nothing. We have to simply take it because there is nothing an individual can do about it and We The People very seldomly band together to demand results. But, in our defense, how can we? If we stop driving then we don't get to work and we don't feed our families (well, the businesses for which we work could allow teleworking to not only boycott gasoline but also save their employees, and themselves, money). So, we trudge on through the BS, taking our licks and either complain about it or "look on the bright side".

My point is this, our "leaders" are charged with making our lives better and they are doing a horrible job. They are stuck in this cycle of doing the bare minimum while continuing to improve their lives. But isn't that the goal? To make your life and family as happy as possible? Maybe we're all suckers for not taking advantage of the weak, stepping on the necks of the less fortunate, or finding all the loopholes designed to make people rich? Possibly, but it just doesn't sit right with me. I expect people to do their job with the same vigor as I do. I expect elected officials to disregard their own time, money, and life for the betterment of this country. That's their job – doing anything less is treason.

Garbage

Another important issue I would deal with is garbage. There must be a better way to "dispose" of garbage than landfills. I know that we recycle some and incinerate others but the most popular method by far is landfills. This doesn't seem very sustainable and a "quick fix" that will someday catch up with us. Also, it's widely known that a great deal of trash ends up in other places besides landfills. Water sources, for instance, are a popular place to find garbage.

I would create a committee of experts to find a better way to really dispose of our garbage. There seems like there should be a safe way to use the energy created by burning the garbage, one that won't result in hazardous smoke contaminating the air. I would scrub all government grants and eliminate the ones that aren't directly contributing to the betterment of the country and use that money to facilitate this and other endeavors. I feel like this isn't being done due to the sheer magnitude of the job. I feel that money is being wasted on frivolous efforts and needs to be identified to either rein in our debt or put it to better use.

Lobbyists

Isn't it odd that we all know the most prevalent problem in Washington, yet nobody does anything about it? I'm talking, of course, about the unscrupulous practice of lobbying. How do we let these vultures into our "most hallowed" halls to negatively influence those who are charged with fighting against these very people?

Everyone complains about the corruption of lobbying, yet it is as ubiquitous as it's ever been. The only explanation is that everyone in Washington who could do anything about it is profiting from it. How else can one explain it? If it is so bad, and such a detriment to the nation, why isn't anyone even attempting to stop it?

This is how you know corporations run this country; they can afford to pay people to stand in line for hours for their lobbyist to bend the ear of those who make policy. The squeaky wheel definitely gets the grease in Washington, as long as it is a very influential, and very wealthy, squeaky wheel.

If I were in charge, I would do everything I could to make it extremely difficult for the lobbyists to continue this behavior. I would push for the most unwelcoming conditions in the waiting areas. I would make the access policy so stringent that it would be almost impossible for them to enter the area. I would make it the most arduous, and undesirable, job in the world and pull back the veil of every hint of impropriety.

I would have teams of investigators kicking over every rock possible to ensure those who are supposed to be working for the people are doing that, and only that. Any self-promotion or self-service will be met with the most stringent and damaging penalties possible. This will deter any ne'er do wells from seeking office in the future and ensure that only those who truly want to improve the way of life of Americans will even run for office.

No lawmaker should be getting rich during their tenure as a public servant. On the contrary, as I've said before, it should be such a grueling endeavor that no one would even consider a second or third term, let alone make a career out of it. People worry about continuity or say ignorant things like "if we vote these people out, we'll only get worse people in there", as if enduring the evil of the current servants is better than taking our chances with new blood. This is madness. The fact that Americans simply vote for a name, or a color is exactly why we continue to suffer from the same enduring problems. The politicians aren't to blame, it is We the People who are to blame for allowing these jackals to remain in "power".

𝔙𝔬𝔱𝔦𝔫𝔤

There seems to be a problem with voting in this country (The U.S.). Even if the system is sound and there is no corruption, human error, suppression, or influence, the current system gives the impression that there is. So how do we correct the system to make it better?

The first thing we should do is streamline the process. If you have a social security number, then you can vote. Only U.S. citizens are supposed to vote so it only makes sense to use everyone's social. This would allow the system to be done all online. Yes, there are chances of hacking but there are ways to combat it, thereby eliminating human error from the process.

Until we move the entire process online, a person should have to show their social security card at the polls along with their personal identification (ID, driver's license, passport, etc.). I believe this would cut down on non-American citizens voting in our elections.

Furthermore, to make it easier for people to vote, all election days should be federal holidays or on the weekend. This would prevent people from having to miss work to vote. It is one of our few civic duties and it should be regarded in a way commensurate with its importance.

Medication

Another initiative I alluded to earlier is making medication affordable and making life-saving medication free. The thought of someone suffering from a life-threatening illness and still having to pay for the very medication they need to live seems abhorrent. I've talked about this in other places, but I firmly believe it should be illegal to profit from something that people need to live.

Now, I know what you're thinking, if people can't make money from the drug, what will motivate them to spend millions of dollars to create and manufacture the drug? This is why the government should be in charge of drug production in this country. They should be in charge of the research and development, creation, and distribution of prescription medication, or at least be a competitor. This would also allow the government to earn profits from the drugs and alleviate some of the tax burden on its citizens.

This is one of many ways the government could earn money aside from tax revenue.

The bottom line, making someone pay anything, let alone exorbitant amounts of money, for drugs they need to live is not right. Every effort should be made to ensure people receive what they need to live a happy life.

Abortion

Instead of abortions, the government will fund the pregnancy and have a waiting list for parents who are unable to have children. Biological mothers will give birth and relinquish all rights to the baby. If biological parents wish to keep their baby, they will repay the government for all pre-natal and natal costs.

Homelessness

Homelessness is a tricky subject because we are all free to live how we want as long as we don't negatively affect others. No one has the right to just take our stuff simply because it is a broken radio in a shopping cart. Some people react to homelessness in an elitist and entitled way by looking down on them, but we don't know their situation and should strive to help rather than condemn.

The first thing to do is take all the IRS workers and convert their positions to a homelessness task force whose only purpose is to find or create places for homeless people to live. They could scout out empty buildings or build their own but finding a place for people to live should be priority number one. The focus should also be individual units to ensure privacy and safety. There should also be larger spaces for single mothers and/or families.

Simultaneously the task force will be finding ways to feed, and provide water to, the homeless. This could entail working with local grocery stores or restaurants to secure edible food that is marked to be discarded and bring that to the homeless. Supplying water could be as simple as running a hose to a "watering station" like you may see at a football practice. The "Sheltering" task force could solicit assistance from local businesses and or non-profits to procure water bottles so patrons could fill them up at the watering stations to take back to their temporary "homes".

After the basics are provided, the task force would find resources for the newly sheltered people like mental health providers, physical health providers, employment counselors, and clothing resources for those who need it.

There could be an on-site office for the providers complete with a full medical staff. Or the shelters could be constructed in close vicinity to a medical facility so the newly sheltered would only have a short walk to receive services.

There should be either a latrine facility constructed or more than enough portable latrines to accommodate all the current and future patrons of the facility.

The goal of this facility is to get people back on their feet and eventually out of the facility and on their own. They should be allowed to stay as long as they want, but strict records should be kept, tracking how long each person has stayed and what services they have used. Eventually, once they start working, they can pay a monthly fee to stay there which may prompt them to move out and find their own place.

In order to facilitate this effort, laws must be passed at the federal and state level with specific language to prevent "homelessness". These laws would be enforced by the new task force so as not to burden local law enforcement with this effort. The IRS offices in each state will be converted to "Sheltering" offices which will allow them to deal with the problem in their vicinity. There should be personnel within the unit who converted from armed IRS law enforcement agents to armed "sheltering task force" agents who police these "newly sheltered" facilities.

𝕲un 𝕾afety

People used to be very comfortable with handling guns in this country, we need to get back to that to not only make guns safer, but also to ensure everyone is able to defend themselves against criminals.

I believe this can be accomplished with federally funded gun safety courses. As it is now, private organizations make money from citizens by teaching them all types of gun handling courses. This seems wrong to me. It seems like there should be federally funded gun courses to ensure the citizens of this country are properly trained to exercise their second amendment right.

I would divert funds, again, from the IRS and use it to hold nationally accredited gun safety courses for all firearm owners. This should actually be mandatory but that may be difficult to enforce unless the gun buyer is made to sit through the training at the time of the sale. This actually wouldn't be a bad idea, it's not like someone needs to buy a gun expeditiously and, if they do, it's probably for nefarious reasons. We could mandate that every firearm dealer and/or salesman be trained in teaching firearm safety (federally funded) and while the gun buyer's background check is being conducted, the salesman could conduct a short but thorough gun safety class to include the four rules of gun safety as well as proper disassembly, cleaning, and reassembly of the weapon. The salesman should also address state and federal self-defense laws to ensure the patron is aware of how and when they can defend themselves. I believe this would prevent many accidental, and intentional, deaths and make for an overall safer community.

Operations Security

A large problem I see with today's military, and government in general, is the lack of operational security. By that I mean too much information has been declassified and too much information about the operation of our military and government can be found in open-source locations. I'm not just talking about rogue web pages that claim to have information, I'm talking about people directly affiliated, or formerly affiliated, with the military and/or government releasing information that could potentially be detrimental to those currently serving.

I don't understand why we let anything out. Specifications of equipment, troop movements, and general operation of our military should be highly classified. Our enemies know too much about what we have and what we do, we shouldn't be making it easier.

Some may say that this is by design, that giving them what we want them to see while classifying what we don't is somehow better, but I disagree. I think we should make them work for every piece of information, no matter how innocuous. This would cause them to be overwhelmed by "classified" information and diminish the chances of them finding out anything truly detrimental to our servicemen and women.

There shouldn't be stories on new gear or vehicles, web pages describing missions, or personal pages with photographic evidence of day-to-day operations. Usually this has been reserved for conventional unit operations but now we know more than we ever did about the special operations community which makes it easier for our enemies to target those elite men and women who are not so easily replaced.

I think our military leaders have become so worried about what the public thinks of the military that they have succumbed to pressure to be more open. Although our "leaders" made some bad choices regarding how to employ troops, I do think their operational security was sound. Clandestine operations were just that and those executing those missions were either a rumor or completely unknown. Now we broadcast the operations of these elite units for the world to see and scrutinize.

The first place to start "locking things down" would be the white house. I realize there are secure spaces there, but it seems there are a lot of leaks that occur from white house employees. This should be stopped and those violating that trust should be severely punished. Only government issued, and tracked, phones should be allowed in those spaces. Only highly vetted personnel should be allowed anywhere near our government's operational area (which is essentially anywhere the president is). There should be a flawless way to know who is leaking what information. All meetings should be compartmentalized, and roll should be taken to ensure we can easily determine who leaked what information based on the nature, location, and topic of the meeting.

𝕷𝖆𝖜𝖘

Federal laws should be the least restrictive and as you get down to the state and local level, those respective governments should have the option to be more restrictive, but not less. As it is now there are federal laws that can't possibly be enforced while the same law has been overturned at the state and/or local level. The federal government should be in charge of issuing laws based on interstate commerce/security/safety, not necessarily an individual's rights. This should be reserved for the states and, actually, at the lowest jurisdiction and/or stringent law where the offence occurred.

As an example, marijuana is still illegal under federal law, yet several states have legalized it. This should never be the case. The federal government should never restrict what a state has deemed legal, just as a state should not restrict what a lower jurisdiction has deemed legal. The power should, at all times, rest with local government. This is where "The People" truly have power.

It's not the federal government's job to take care of you. That responsibility lies directly with you. However, if a person chooses to live within a society, they will need others at some point. But these others should not, usually, be at the federal level. Your local community's job is to take care of those in their community.

That's where this whole country began, little pockets of people in a community, or "tribe", if you will. A group of people that looked out for each other and helped each other. They planted crops, built houses, and shared responsibilities within their small circles.

You shouldn't be relying on the federal government to help you. We need to bring more power back to the local government and then work out from there.

When I say I would like to run for president, it has nothing to do with me wanting to be powerful or famous.

The way I look at it is the President of the United States is the least important person on this planet because this whole job is to take care of all the people under him. This means empowering state and local governments to implement laws that suit those in that community.

The state and local government (which are really over the federal government in the grand scheme of things), and the federal government should be working tirelessly to assure that every American has everything they need to be successful and happy. At the time of this writing, and in recent history, this has not been happening. We haven't had a president that represented the people since Reagan and, frankly, before that. Maybe Lincoln or Teddy Roosevelt. These men seemed selfless, like they only cared about what was right for the country. We need to get back to that and allow communities to decide what is best for them and keep the federal government out of it.

𝔅𝔲𝔡𝔤𝔢𝔱 ℭ𝔲𝔱𝔰

Federal Programs to reduce and/or eliminate to cut and/or redirect spending.

- Programs to cut/reduce:

  o U.S. Geological Survey: $680M annually

  o Rural Housing Development Service: $400M annually

  o Small Business Administration: $660M annually

  o Natural Resource Conservation Service: $700M annually

  o The Public Health Svc Commission Corps $125M annually

  o Davis-Bacon Act (TITLE 40, USC) $1.8B annually

  o ACDA section of the State Department $8M annually

  o Corporation for Public Broadcasting $260M annually

  o Economic Development Administration $186M annually

  o Social Security Administration $260B annually

  o Repeal ACA exchange subsidies $105B annually

o Eliminate Non-Medicaid State Health Grants $172B annually

o Eliminate DOA Farm/Food/Rural Subsidies $184B annually

o Eliminate DOC telecom/economic dev subs $5B annually

o Eliminate college student aid $90B annually

o Eliminate DOE subsidies $6.8B annually

o Dissolve TSA (airport responsibility) $5.3B annually

o Dissolve FEMA (state responsibility) $24B annually

o End HUD Rental Assistance $40B annually

o End HUD Comm Dev subsidies $19B annually

o Dept of Interior net outlay reduction/elimination $10-20B annually

o Eliminate DOJ state/local disc grants $2.6B annually

o Eliminate DOT urban transit subsidies $21B annually

o Eliminate DOT highway aid that exceeds $19B annually

o fuel tax revenues

- o Privatize Amtrak and end rail subsidies $7B annually

- o Eliminate Dept of Treas Tax credits $89B annually

- o Cut/Eliminate Foreign Aid $12-24B annually

- o Eliminate EPA grants $3B annually

Save $500B by following the GAO's advice annotated here:

https://www.gao.gov/blog/where-can-government-save-money-weve-found-more-half-trillion-dollars-potential-savings?fbclid=IwAR3Iei9njOBzUrzp_JzmIgtX_eVvL6rO3l1jBxKxuposl_11m8rz3uCDYFo

- o The Department of Energy could pursue less expensive disposal options of nuclear and hazardous waste, such as immobilizing waste in grout, which could help save tens of billions of dollars.

- o Contracting leaders at federal agencies should use metrics measuring cost reduction or avoidance to improve the performance of their procurement organizations and potentially save billions of dollars annually.

o Congress should consider directing the Department of Health and Human Services to implement additional payment reductions for Skilled Nursing Facilities with high rates of potentially preventable hospital readmissions and emergency room visits, potentially saving hundreds of millions of dollars in Medicare costs.

o The Internal Revenue Service could improve taxpayer service and better manage refund interest payments, potentially saving $20 million or more annually, by establishing a mechanism to identify, monitor, and mitigate issues contributing to refund interest payments.

o The Social Security Administration could potentially save millions of dollars by identifying and addressing the causes for overpayments to disability beneficiaries in its Ticket to Work program.

- o The Department of Defense could improve various administrative services, such as by better managing fragmentation in its food program and strengthening ongoing initiatives to reduce improper defense travel payments, potentially saving millions of dollars in those programs.

Implement the Holman Rule to hold public servants accountable for their actions, or lack of action.

GAO Report to Congressional Addressees:

https://www.gao.gov/assets/730/720470.pdf

New Opportunities Exist to Improve Efficiency and Effectiveness across the Federal Government

https://files.gao.gov/reports/GAO-22-105301/index.html

Table 1: New Fragmentation, Overlap, and Duplication Areas Identified in This Report

Defense

1. DOD's Congressional Reporting Process: The Department of Defense's Office of the Assistant Secretary of Defense for Legislative Affairs should consult with internal stakeholders and identify opportunities to better manage duplication and fragmentation in its congressional reporting process.

2. DOD Food Program Costs: The Department of Defense should assess the effectiveness and efficiency of its food program, as well as identify and define specific categories of costs for use in developing common measures to better manage fragmentation in its food program and potentially save millions of dollars annually.

3. DOD Nuclear Enterprise Oversight: The Department of Defense should clearly identify roles and responsibilities, among other steps, to improve coordination and better manage fragmentation among its new nuclear oversight

organization and other nuclear oversight groups and stakeholders.

Energy

4. DOI's Oil and Gas Data Systems: The Department of the Interior could better manage fragmentation and potential duplication by implementing a plan to address challenges with the key data systems it uses to manage oil and gas development, resulting in improved oversight and saved staff time.

General Government

5. Drug Control Grant Tracking: The Office of National Drug Control Policy should document its process for identifying duplication, overlap, and fragmentation among drug control grants to better manage fragmented grant efforts, retain organizational knowledge, and demonstrate its internal control system's effectiveness.

6. Trade-Based Money Laundering: The Departments of the Treasury and Homeland Security could better manage

fragmentation among their departments and other agencies with trade enforcement responsibilities and better detect illicit financial and trade activity by taking actions to enhance information sharing.

Health

7. Diet-Related Chronic Health Conditions: Congress should consider identifying and directing a federal entity to lead a federal strategy for reducing diet-related chronic health conditions, which could help manage fragmentation and overlap across 200 federal programs and activities.

8. Medicaid Behavioral Health Demonstration: The Centers for Medicare & Medicaid Services should issue clear and consistent guidance to states participating in the certified community behavioral health clinics demonstration to help avoid potential duplication between demonstration payments and other Medicaid payments.

Homeland Security/Law Enforcement

9. Alternative Technologies for Radioactive Materials: Congress could help better manage fragmentation between the relevant agencies and mitigate potential fiscal exposure to the federal government from accidental or intentional incidents by directing the establishment of a national strategy for replacing technologies that use high-risk radioactive materials with alternatives.

10. Biodefense Preparedness and Response: Federal and non-federal entities have opportunities to better prepare for and respond to significant biological incidents, including to better manage fragmented federal efforts.

11. Law Enforcement's Use of Force: The Department of Justice should analyze use of force data collection efforts to identify the extent of potential overlap, validate these findings using relevant information, and identify options to better manage any existing overlap.

Information Technology

12. Digital Service Guidance: The Office of Management and Budget and General Services Administration could better manage fragmentation and reduce the risk of overlapping and duplicating efforts in developing information technology guidance for federal agencies by improving coordination between their U.S. Digital Service and 18F programs.

13. Farm Production and Conservation IT Duplication and Overlap: By developing a strategic plan with performance goals and measures, the U.S. Department of Agriculture's Farm Production and Conservation mission area could maximize efficiencies and reduce IT duplication and overlap.

Science and the Environment

14. Emergency Watershed Protection: The U.S. Department of Agriculture should clarify and document roles and responsibilities for Emergency Watershed Protection projects on National Forest System lands to help address fragmentation and ensure sponsors design the most effective projects.

15. High-Performance Computing: The Office of Science and Technology Policy could better manage fragmentation in federal efforts to advance high-performance computing by fully incorporating desirable characteristics of a national strategy.

16. Nuclear Waste Cleanup Research and Development Efforts: By following leading practices for collaboration, the Department of Energy could better manage fragmentation and reduce potential duplication and overlap in its research and development to address its nuclear waste cleanup mission.

Table 2: New Areas with Cost Savings and Revenue Enhancement Opportunities Identified in This Report

Defense

17. F-35 Lightning II Sustainment: The Department of Defense could reduce F-35 sustainment costs by hundreds of millions, or even billions, of dollars over several years by

developing a strategic approach to ensure that the services can afford to operate and support the F-35.

General Government

18. Federal Contracting Metrics: Contracting leaders at federal agencies should use metrics measuring cost reduction or avoidance to improve the performance of their procurement organizations and potentially save billions of dollars annually.

Health

19. Staffing and Critical Incidents in Medicare Skilled Nursing Facilities: Congress should consider directing the Department of Health and Human Services to implement additional payment reductions for Skilled Nursing Facilities with high rates of potentially preventable hospital readmissions and emergency room visits, potentially saving hundreds of millions of dollars to Medicare.

Homeland Security/Law Enforcement

20. BOP Emergency Preparedness and Response: The Bureau of Prisons should take steps to establish and incorporate cost-effective and feasible analytic features into its data systems and use these features to regularly conduct an analysis of its maintenance and repair project trends, which could save hundreds of thousands of dollars.

Social Services

21. Social Security Disability Payments: The Social Security Administration could potentially save millions of dollars by identifying and addressing the causes for overpayments to Ticket to Work participants.

Source: GAO. | GAO-22-105301

34 new actions related to nine existing areas presented in the GAO 2011 to 2021 annual reports

Table 3: New Actions Added to Existing Areas in 2022

Defense

Department of Defense Commissaries and Exchanges' In February 2022, GAO identified one new action to help the Department of Defense better manage fragmentation among its commissaries and exchanges by establishing an overarching policy and more consistent processes to provide reasonable assurance that its resale goods are not produced by forced labor.

Defense Travel: In June 2021, GAO identified one new action to help the Department of Defense strengthen its ongoing initiatives to reduce improper travel payments, potentially saving millions of dollars over 5 years.

Economic Development

Economic Development Programs: In July 2021, GAO identified five new actions to help the Departments of

Commerce, Housing and Urban Development, and Agriculture incorporate further collaboration to help grantees and local communities better manage fragmented efforts related to federal economic development.

Energy
• DOE's Treatment of Hanford's Low Activity Waste In December 2021, GAO identified three new actions to help save tens of billions of dollars by allowing the Department of Energy to pursue less expensive disposal options. 2018

• Oil and Gas Resources: In November 2021, GAO identified two new actions to help the Bureau of Land Management improve its oil and gas leasing process, which could potentially result in millions of dollars in additional revenues over the next decade. 2011

General Government
Department of Veterans Affairs Medical Facility Construction: In October 2021, GAO identified two new actions to help the Department of Veterans Affairs avoid schedule delays and better manage medical facility

construction projects by improving communication between offices.

IRS Taxpayer Service: In April 2022, GAO identified three new actions to help IRS improve taxpayer service and better manage refund interest payments, potentially saving $20 million or more annually.

Spectrum Management: In June 2021, GAO identified eight new actions to enhance coordination between the two agencies that manage radio-frequency spectrum—a scarce natural resource—to better manage fragmentation.

Social Services
Homelessness Programs: In September 2021, GAO identified nine new actions for federal agencies to coordinate youth homelessness information and programs in order to manage fragmented services to better support communities.

Source: GAO. | GAO-22-105301

a) The area named Department of Defense Commissaries and Exchanges was formerly named Department of Defense

Commissaries. The area name is being changed to fully reflect the one new action that is being added in 2022.

b) One of the new actions being added to this area replaces one of the existing actions. The current potential financial benefits from these actions remain consistent with prior reporting.

Congress and Executive Branch Agencies Continue to Address Actions Identified over the Last 12 Years across the Federal Government, Resulting in Significant Benefits

Congress and executive branch agencies have made consistent progress in addressing many of the actions we have identified since 2011, as shown in figure 2 and table 4. As of March 2022, Congress and executive branch agencies had fully or partially addressed 964 (about 74 percent) of the 1,299 actions; of these, they had fully addressed 724 and partially addressed 240 actions. See GAO's online Action Tracker for the status of all actions.

From the CATO Institute:

https://www.cato.org/blog/what-federal-spending-cut-0

- Medicare. Congress should increase premiums and cost-sharing while moving to a system of vouchers to encourage competition and cost control.

- Medicaid. Congress should convert federal aid to block grants in order to cut federal spending and encourage state innovation and cost reductions.

- Defense. The largest federal bureaucracy is the Pentagon's civilian staff of 750,000. A Washington Post investigation suggested that bloat in the defense bureaucracy cost more than $100 billion year. I don't know whether that is true, but the Pentagon could certainly save money by tackling excessive layering, cost overruns, and corruption.

- Interest. Without reforms, interest costs are expected to double over the next seven years, but those costs would fall if Congress cut spending.

- Other Spending. Congress should cut food subsidies, farm subsidies, energy subsidies, housing subsidies, rural subsidies, development subsidies, K 12 subsidies, college subsidies, welfare subsidies, disaster subsidies, security subsidies, community subsidies, developer subsidies, water subsidies, grazing subsidies, unemployment subsidies, training subsidies, highway subsidies, transit subsidies, airport subsidies, rail subsidies, worker subsidies, foreign aid subsidies, business subsidies, flood subsidies, power subsidies, and much more.

Other Initiatives:

- Stop making pennies and nickels - $95M annually
- Only make dollar coins, stop making dollar bills - $184M

From US News & World Report:

https://www.usnews.com/news/articles/2011/05/26/eight-easy-ways-to-cut-government-spending?fbclid=IwAR0f0aH_Rwey9dfnkAFHZqBLx1imZj_xycKBn3RkuC_6rpY2eGXevsDYv5M

- Stop Mailing a Record of Everything that the Government Does - $4M
- Stop Printing everything congress says - $8M
- Stop the Specialty Crop Block Grant Program - $55M
- Cut USPS mail delivery to five times a week - $3B OR, Privatize the USPS
- Whenever possible, federal employees work from home.
- Cut federal work week to four days.
  - Saves government money by not using as much energy (lights, computers, phones, etc.)
  - Reduces carbon emissions
  - Saves employees money by not having to buy as much fuel for
  - their cars

From Brookings:

https://www.brookings.edu/interactives/15-ways-to-rethink-the-federal-budget-2/?fbclid=IwAR3KUgCCnkliOE6RyIRrcn3j5RW-euWZyEjA_v4R4mZa6zNNQR2uzWQcF4g

- Transitioning to Bundled Payments in Medicare - $100B

- Reforming Federal Support for Risky Development - $40B

- Restructuring Cost Sharing and Supplemental Insurance for

- Medicare - $125B

- An Evidence-Based Path to Disability Insurance Reform - $20B

- Eliminating Fossil Fuel Subsidies - $41B

- Replacing the Home Mortgage Interest Deduction - $300B

- Funding Transportation Infrastructure with User Fees - $312B

- Creating an American Value-Added Tax - $1.6T

- Overhauling the Temporary Work Visa System - $12B

- Increasing the Role of the Private Sector in Housing Finance -

- $134B

From the Washington Post:

https://www.washingtonpost.com/wp-srv/interactivity/what-would-you-cut.html?fbclid=IwAR0eNxq5GQtfAYA7jkEIn0I68YZognrOTyX1ZXxeolO2Ay-hzeg20rV2NTs

Actual submissions:

Streamline the EPA: Management. The layers of management are insane...it takes thirteen steps and five layers to get a signature from our Office Director, more to get a signature to the Assistant Secretary/Administrator. --EPA employee

The National Park Service--specifically it's management of "recreation areas." We have the Forest Service, we have BLM, Army Corps and who knows who else all managing mixed use federal land. But when the NPS is thrown into urban recreation management? Well of a course a 2400-page action plan on dog poop results...--Retired federal employee

The DOJ Antitrust Division and the FTC both have antitrust departments. They also both have groups of people whose sole job is to fight with the other on who get to oversee what mergers. --Washington, DC

The Department of Labor proposed rules last year to weed out for-profit schools that are reaping huge profits from federal student loan programs but are clearly incapable of producing graduates who will have the earning power to repay their loans. The standards the department proposed were -- from a taxpayer's perspective -- ridiculously low. Even if only 35% of a school's graduates are paying back their loans, the school would remain eligible to receive funds from student loans under the DOL plan. Unfortunately, since many schools, including the Washington Post Company's Kaplan College, can't even meet that joke of a standard, the industry's response has been to launch a lobbying effort to keep the student loan funds flowing into their coffers. This seems to have caused some members Congress who claim to be looking diligently for ways to cut the budget to look right past the $10 billion or so in annual savings that they could have achieved by simply telling the DOL to implement the rules they wrote last year without changes. —exco

"Pay increases accorded for longevity should be abolished, replaced with a hybrid system of

1) COLAs [Cost of Living Adjustments]: everybody gets these, as funding allows and

2) Merit pay increases: based on merit, as funding allows, and after all COLAs are paid. In addition, promotions shouldn't require a mountain of paperwork, and terminations shouldn't, either." --Seattle, WA

"Foreign Aid. All in some cases and some in all cases. IE Pakistan, Middle East Countries who are oil producers. The state department also needs deeper cuts. Economic aid to other countries can't be happening if our country is going to end up something similar. Get our own finances straight and then you can spread peace on earth." –Unknown

The IRS comprises several divisions, each headed by executives. Each division comprises several offices (in my own division, there are 11), also headed by executives. Within each office are further units or functions, with managers who lead other managers, who – in many cases – lead other managers. Bottom line, there are way too many levels of management, too many executives, too much duplication of effort, too many meetings, etc. We simply have too much "managing" going on: meetings about meetings, time spent fine-tuning the administration of the organization, and so on. We could greatly reduce our budget by simplifying the management areas of responsibility, thereby reducing the executive and upper-level management ranks. We also have too many employees (many of them in higher pay brackets) in the administrative areas, and too few in the field, assisting taxpayers. (By the way, I work in headquarters, so I don't say this out of malice, but based on first-hand observation.) We could accomplish reducing the payroll at the administrative end through simple attrition. Many employees and managers in those offices are at or near retirement age. These would also be some of the higher grades. Some employees may be reluctant to retire in these perilous times but buy-outs would get things moving. We could achieve significant payroll reduction in 5-7 years. It's even possible that we could save enough to increase hiring in field positions, where more help is needed. The difficulty, of course, is that headquarters is also where these decisions are made. Executives are understandably hesitant to cut their own throats, or those of their colleagues. It's much easier to slash the payroll of those guys "out there," or to cut the non-payroll budget. --IRS Employee

A BBC news report stated that USAID has made a grant of $20 million to Rafi Peer Theater group to create a local version of Sesame Street. This isn't just translating Sesame Street into Pakistani, it's creating Pakistani characters. I'm sure an argument can be made for this, but doesn't it seem that we should go through the entire budget and eliminate unnecessary programs, given that we're borrowing $1.6 trillion a year for these programs? --Benson

**State Department must make a valid argument for all USAID expenditures.

Non-Tax Revenue

It seems like a very flimsy, and unethical, business model to rely on taxes to generate income for the government. This is why the government is so concerned with the unemployment rate. The lower the unemployment rate, the more taxes (theoretically) the government can collect. But what if people don't work? What if the amount of taxes collected isn't sufficient to run the government? You know, like now.

There must be a better way for the government to generate revenue. I think it's very lazy, and extremely unpredictable, to rely on taxing the citizens of the nation to pay for all government programs.

Instead, we should be investing money in a very lucrative hedge fund. Our government officials already make money off the stock market, why doesn't the government change the law so our lawmakers can't make money by insider trading, but they can generate money for the government by researching, and investing, our funds in a successful hedge fund, or other investment? Private investors make billions on these funds, why shouldn't the federal government? Yes, I'm sure someone will try, and/or succeed, in corrupting this system for their own gain but at least the people of this country will not have to pay as many taxes as they have in the past. The government manipulating the system to make money from the stock market, which would pay for government programs that help Americans, and Americans are no longer responsible, seems like a win/win situation. This seems more like what our government should be doing instead of what they have been doing which is conducting shady activity that is a detriment to Americans.

We could also buy real estate here, and in other countries, maybe around some ports or other areas that we can charge for utilization. One thing the Chinese are doing that makes sense to me is spreading their influence around the world but in a non-military way. They're investing in ports, mines, and energy-creating facilities like the geothermal facility they just purchased in Alaska.

What about gambling? Making gambling illegal is another one of those efforts that make no sense, other than "big brother" trying to look out for you so you don't lose all your money. But it's legal in so many other places, why not all? And why not government owned? This would cut out the middleman. As of now, the government taxes your winnings, but what if they received your losses instead? Gambling losses far outweigh gambling wins.

Other Initiatives

- Every purchase an American makes is rounded up to the nearest dollar and given to the government.

- Sales tax on all "non-essential" items.

- Flat tax for all Americans (this would eliminate the need for a robust IRS, leaving those positions and money to go to other things, like the border.)

- Federal legalization of gambling. Tax all gambling establishments on their "winnings", regardless of non-profit status. Eliminate tax on individual Americans' winnings.

- Invest in lucrative hedge funds, stocks, etc.

- Purchase profitable real estate around the globe like ports, mining operations, etc.

- Either increase the corporate tax rate or turn over "government programs" to corporations to run.
  - Also, require corporations to make a significant contribution to each community they affect. E.g., the

Microsoft Foster Home, the Amazon Community

Center, the Tesla Public Library

o Or simply aid low-income neighborhood schools.

Low-income neighborhood schools will never

overcome their adversity without changing how we

(The U.S.) does things. The current structure is not

working.

o Give incentives for manufacturing products in the

U.S.

o Heavy import tax on all "non-essential" items.

- Slowly, and safely, convert all power to nuclear while

continuing to extract U.S. based fossil fuels.

o Retain rights to all drilling/excavating operations and

use these rights to generate revenue.

- Go through the federal budget line-by-line and cut all

non-essential expenditures. Some temporarily, some

permanently. For example. The $1.144B given to the

Smithsonian could have been used to secure the

southern border.

- Legalize, regulate, and heavily tax all "illegal" substances to:

  o Generate revenue

  o Reduce OD and other drug related deaths due to unregulated products

  o Reduce/Eliminate violence in/around the southern U.S. border and in the U.S.

EPILOGUE

It's indisputable that this country has become something almost unrecognizable from what our forefathers created. They established an almost perfect construct to serve the people however, like most things in this world, that near-perfect construct has eroded into something that really only serves the ultra-rich and powerful and actually hinders and/or hurts the people.

The only true way to correct this is to start from scratch by voting out all incumbents, abolishing political parties, and strengthening local government. The federal government was never meant to be as overreaching and intrusive as it has become. It needs to be reduced to its original form and solely focus on country-wide issues.

Unfortunately, it seems like this will be our reality for the foreseeable future. This means that local government has never been more vital. The federal government does not have the manpower to enforce countrywide legislation so, local governments need only exercise silent non-compliance in order to do what is right for their citizens. It's already happening around the country, state and local governments are exercising their freedom by making decisions based on their citizen's wishes instead of outdated or unjust federal laws.

If I were to be elected President, I would do everything I could to reduce the federal government's influence in state and local issues, find ways to generate revenue to reduce/eliminate taxes on our citizens, and take extreme measure to ensure our country was safe from all threats. If you'd like to discuss any of this further, please contact me at Jarrod@tryitlikethis.net.

You may not do everything you want in life,

but do everything you can.

About the Author

Jarrod Welsh

Jarrod Welsh retired from the US Air Force after ~24 years of service, over half being with special operations. Following his retirement he worked in Child Protection for two years and is currently a military contractor. He and his wife also write children's books and have four children.

Twitter: @TryItLikeThis
IG: @jarrod_TryItLikeThis
FB: @TryItLikeThis
Web: tryitlikethis.net

www.ingramcontent.com/pod-product-compliance
Lightning Source LLC
Chambersburg PA
CBHW050112280326
41933CB00010B/1066